THE STORY OF
DAVID BEN-GURION

Ben Gurion

The Story of

DAVID
BEN-GURION

by

BARNET LITVINOFF

LONDON

VALLENTINE, MITCHELL

First published 1960 by
Vallentine, Mitchell & Co. Ltd., 37 Furnival Street, London, E.C. 4

FOR ADRIAN AND MILES

Made and printed in Great Britain
by C. Tinling & Co. Ltd.
Liverpool, London and Prescot

Contents

Map of Israel on page 8

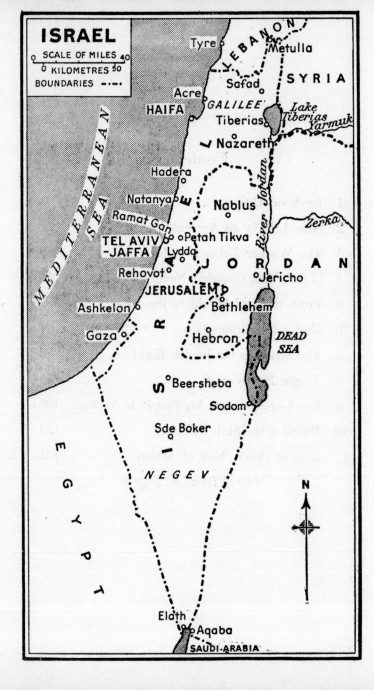

ISRAEL

SCALE OF MILES
KILOMETRES
BOUNDARIES -·-·-

MEDITERRANEAN SEA

LEBANON

Tyre

Metulla

SYRIA

Safad

Acre

GALILEE

Lake Tiberias

HAIFA

Tiberias

Yarmuk

Nazareth

River Jordan

Hadera

Natanya

Nablus

Zerka

Ramat Gan

TEL AVIV
-JAFFA

Petah Tikva

Lydda

JORDAN

Rehovot

Jericho

JERUSALEM

Ashkelon

Bethlehem

DEAD
SEA

Gaza

Hebron

Beersheba

Sodom

Sde Boker

NEGEV

N

EGYPT

Elath

Aqaba

SAUDI ARABIA

CHAPTER ONE

Boyhood Dreams

IT was like a clap of thunder, shaking the little market-town of Plonsk, in Poland, out of what might have been an age-long sleep.

A lawyer named Avigdor Green, and his friends, had started the rumpus by talking about Zionism. They wanted the Jews to do something to change their way of life as they had known it for centuries past. They said that Palestine must be regarded not merely as the land of the Bible, but as a real Jewish homeland again, as it was when they were a nation in ancient times.

The year was 1880. People clustered in knots at the street-corners to hear what the Zionists had to say, or stayed late at the Synagogue. The lawyer argued that the Jews had been despised too long in Europe. They ought to be ashamed because their neighbours did not look upon them as equals.

"Let us speak our ancient tongue of Hebrew again!" he urged. "This will be the first step towards making us a free people."

What was this? muttered some of the wise old

9

men of Plonsk. Who dared to preach about a return
of the Jews to Palestine? Where would this talk about
the holy tongue being a language for everyday use
lead them? These were dangerous ideas, and they
stood up in the Synagogue and shook their fists at
Avigdor Green. He was a trouble-maker, they said,
and must be stopped.

But the lawyer stood his ground. "We've lived too
long in the ghetto," he exclaimed. "Times are changing, yet we're still in the Middle Ages. No wonder
we are despised and persecuted!"

Luckily, the Zionists found a champion in one of
the leading rabbis of Plonsk, the highly-respected
Simcha Isaac. "Avigdor is right," he said. "There is
no future for our children in the Russian Empire. We
have no rights here."

This was indeed the case. Jews were not given
equality before the law in those days. They were
often forced to pay extra taxes, they could only work
at special trades, and had to live within a certain
area, called the Pale of Settlement. If they tried to
leave it without permission, they ran the danger of
severe punishment.

You could tell a Jew in the Pale of Settlement
because of his style of dress, and the Yiddish he
generally spoke, and his extremely religious way of
life. But Avigdor Green had never been afraid to
look over the walls of the ghetto. He was curious
about the wider world outside, and he soon found
that the Jews of Poland lagged far behind their
neighbours, Jewish as well as Gentile. In Germany,
for example, the Jews had won self-respect and

equality a hundred years earlier, under the great thinker Moses Mendelssohn. Then why should not the same privileges be theirs too?

Of course, the Emperor, who was known as the Czar, had his spies, his secret police, if there was trouble from the Jews. This meant that the lawyer and his friends had to go quietly about the task of spreading their Zionist ideas. And they made progress, even though there was some shaking of old Jewish heads, who taught that it was wrong to think of Palestine as a homeland until the Messiah, in his own good time, came to lead them back to Jerusalem.

Avigdor Green made his house the headquarters of the Zionist movement in Plonsk. From his frequent visits to Warsaw, Poland's capital, he brought back newspapers printed in Hebrew, and prominent men to talk about their plans.

It was natural, therefore, for his ideas to take firmest root in his own home, which was the place where the poor Jews of Plonsk would come with their problems every day. One day, in 1886, there was a large gathering of people waiting to see him, but the lawyer seemed more than usually busy. When he did appear, they all tried to talk at once.

"Reb Avigdor," one of them said, "my cow has been stolen. Can you bring the thief to court?" And before the answer came another asked for an urgent letter to be written. "They have called me to the army, Reb Avigdor, and I must ask the authorities to make provision for my wife." Yet a third joined the chorus. "Our rabbi has gone to Warsaw, Reb Avigdor. Please help us to choose a new one."

Smiling, the lawyer silenced them with a gesture. "Now I have something important to tell you, my friends. My dear wife Sheindal has just given birth to our sixth child, a son. We shall call him David."

Yes, Zionism *did* take root in the Green household. This child was destined, 66 years later, to become the first Prime Minister of Israel, the Jewish State.

Rabbi Simcha Isaac was among the first to hurry to Avigdor's home to bring his good wishes. For their common faith in Zionism had turned them into great friends.

"My blessings upon you and your dear wife," said the rabbi. "Your boy will see great changes in our people. Of that you may be sure."

"I shall prepare him for those changes," Avigdor replied. "My son David will learn to speak Hebrew. He will study at the religious school, of course, but he must learn history too, and get to understand the world."

As a boy David was small for his age. He had dark eyes and hair. By the time he could walk he showed that he was no ordinary child. At six he played a good game of chess. Within a year or two after that he became passionately fond of reading, and he was a most attentive listener whenever his elders discussed the important matters of the day.

And with all this he was a devoted son. He showed a special love for his mother, and she in return lavished every care upon his up-bringing. Sheindal's was a hard life, even for those days. In addition to all the help she had to give her husband in his work as a lawyer and a Zionist, there was David and his many brothers and sisters to keep her busy. Unhappily, only six of the eleven children she bore lived to grow up.

David Green was born at a time when Zionism itself was in its infancy, without great leaders, and with only the vaguest idea of how its aims could be achieved. What it needed was a man of action. It was not long before such a man came upon the scene. His name was Theodor Herzl.

This remarkable man was to change the direction of the boy's life. He was a Viennese writer who came to Zionism by a roundabout way. Herzl had been present when Captain Dreyfus was brought to trial in Paris on the faked charge of selling military secrets to Germany, was found guilty and was condemned to long imprisonment on Devil's Island off the coast of South America.

Dreyfus was a Jew, and it was because of this that he had become the target of suspicion and the innocent victim of one of the most notorious trials in history. What Herzl saw filled him with a burning desire to win justice for his people.

Herzl had until then lived quite happily as what you might call a citizen of the world, with important friends in every European capital, and a leading reputation as a journalist. But now he suddenly realised that the Jews were, in fact, defenceless against their enemies. They had no country of their own. Eventually he set down his ideas for such a homeland in a little book called *The Jewish State*, published in 1896. Not content with this, he called together a conference of Zionists from all parts of the world. It was held in Basle, Switzerland, in 1897.

David Green was by then eleven, and not too young to look to the fiery Jewish visionary as his prophet and leader. He obtained the reports of the Zionist Congress and read them over and over again. During the next few years he followed every move his hero took towards furthering their cause.

"Herzl has been to London, and established a Jewish bank there!" he told his friends in wonderment.

"Is such a thing possible?" they asked. "Can a Jew be so important that he can have discussions with leaders of nations, and create a bank in the richest city of the world?"

"This Jew can," David retorted. "Look, he has been to Turkey, and talked with the Sultan. He really is a leader. Our people will follow him in their millions."

This is exactly what happened. Herzl cast a magic spell upon Jewry. Hope ran high, for he spoke with authority, as does a man with great confidence in himself and his ideas. But perhaps hope ran a little too high, for Zionism was still a long way from its goal.

David had two special friends in Plonsk. They were schoolmates with whom he would go off for a bathe in the little river that flowed through the town, or watch the cartloads of grain being heaped into the freight-trains for marketing in Warsaw. One of these, Shlomo Zemach, came from a fairly wealthy family. The other was Shmuel Fuchs, a boy some years older than the others, but their bosom friend just the same.

All three were deeply impressed by the talk they

heard of Herzl and his ambitions for their people. In their young minds the handsome Jewish leader became a super-man, capable of moving mountains in the task he had taken upon himself. They could not understand that Zionism had only just started its long struggle, with many storms and conflicts ahead before the path leading the Jews back to the Promised Land could be cleared.

When David was eleven a tragic blow struck the Green family. Sheindal, the devoted mother and wife, died. She passed away while giving birth to her eleventh child, and a shadow fell on what had till then been a happy household. Avigdor, broken-hearted, drew his children around him and told them that henceforth he would be both father and mother to them.

"You have lost the most precious of God's gifts, a mother's love," he said. "Now our family must keep together, and help to keep this home of ours what it has always been in the past."

Throughout the Jewish quarter of Plonsk the word spread of Sheindal Green's death. People wondered whether the bereaved husband would be able to carry on his work for Zionism and for the poor. He soon gave his answer by his actions. Avigdor laboured with redoubled energy for the cause and, in addition, took an even greater hand in his children's education.

As for David, grief drove him to a silence out of which he refused to emerge for days. Neither his friends nor his father could solace him, so great was his sorrow. And although he was still a boy and at the beginning of his education, it marked the end of his childhood.

After his mother's death David looked for some useful activity. The man who helped him most as he groped around for a way to restore the meaning to his life was none other than his father's old friend, Rabbi Simcha Isaac.

By the time he was fourteen, the boy had recovered sufficiently to throw himself heart and soul into the Zionist movement. With the support of the venerable rabbi and together with his friends Shlomo Zemach and Shmuel Fuchs and his elder brother Abraham, he founded a society of Young Zionists that was soon joined by many of the boys and girls of the town. They planned discussions and readings. They studied politics. Out of their pocket-money they collected funds to send to the Zionist headquarters in Odessa, just as their elders did.

What would they call themselves? It was a strongly-debated point. They knew they had to go to the Bible for a name, for they saw in it the inspiration of all their work. Their reading told them of the return to Zion in ancient days, after the Babylonian captivity, and the part played in rebuilding the temple by Ezra. Surely there was a great similarity between those times and their newly-born hope for Palestine? So they called themselves by the name of Ezra.

As for David's part, this was easily decided. He became their first public speaker and debater. David Green was a born orator. His tongue could be sharp and bitter; he was clever at argument, and he knew the Bible so well that his Zionist speeches were like the sermons of the cleverest rabbis.

The members of Ezra did not think about Zionism alone. Their thoughts were never far away from the injustices of the Czar's Government, from the hunger and poverty that came with the cruelties of their rulers. Could they work for a new Jewish nation without making sure that these evils would not exist in Palestine? Certainly not! Thus it was that they became Socialists also.

Socialist Zionists took a Hebrew term for their cause. It was called 'Poale Zion', meaning the Workers of Zion. David Green has been a member of Poale Zion for the whole of his life.

The boy from Plonsk was growing up to discover that Zionism was to have many ups and downs before it reached its goal. Herzl was learning the same lesson. Like Moses before him, the Zionist leader found that it was not easy to lead the people to the Promised Land. They were impatient with him, at what they considered were high-handed methods.

Herzl had had a most disappointing interview with the Sultan of Turkey, and when he came to report to the Zionist Congress each year he had to confess that progress was very slow indeed. On one occasion Herzl did bring back a scheme from London, where the British Government offered the Jews a home in East Africa. But he was howled down. Most of the Zionists drew their beliefs from their study of the Bible. They would not hear of a Jewish home anywhere but in Palestine.

In this atmosphere of moodiness and disappointment for Jewry, the twentieth century dawned. Many thousands of those who felt hemmed in by the unfriendliness of Eastern Europe sought a way of escape. America lured large numbers to its shores. Some even succeeded, by legal or illegal means, in reaching Palestine. The journey was dangerous, and meant many days of travel to a Mediterranean or Black Sea port. Then came the problem of persuading some ship's captain to take them on to Jaffa, the only fair-sized port in the Holy Land. Even then they had to smuggle themselves ashore, because it was very difficult to get permission from the Turkish authorities to land.

You had to be tough and obstinate to choose the road to Palestine when the majority were making for the New World; but it could be done.

David, too, resolved to go away. When he was 17 he told his father that he wished to continue his studies in Warsaw, which was at that time one of the great cities of Europe, with its splendid palaces and great bridges spanning the Vistula. The idea worried Avigdor, who suspected that his son, with his well-known Socialist views, would get into trouble.

"What will you do in Warsaw?" he asked the youth.

"I shall study and prepare myself for the University," answered his son. "And work for Zionism."

"But you have no money!"

"Others have managed, so shall I," was the reply. "Perhaps I can earn my keep as a Hebrew teacher, or by doing other odd jobs."

Finally the father consented. As David boarded the train, full of hopes and plans, he heard that Theodor Herzl, the man he admired above all others, had become desperately ill.

For the Jewish student, accustomed to the sheltered schooling in a small town, Warsaw was like a voyage of discovery. David entered the city's political life with zest. He found that many Jews were Socialists but not Zionists; some were Zionists but not Socialists; and still more were neither. He attracted the attention of the Poale Zion leaders by his forthright manner, his fighting speeches, his readiness to take on the humblest of duties. But he also attracted the attention of other people: the Czar's secret police, for example.

In a matter of months David Green was caught by the police as a Jewish trouble-maker, and they clapped him into jail. This sort of thing was a not uncommon event in Warsaw. Every so often the police would swoop down on a noisy student gathering, and bundle off the ring-leaders. Generally, you could buy your freedom on the payment of a fine. But David had not the money for such luxuries; and he sent an urgent call to his father for help.

Luckily, Avigdor knew the ins and outs of the law. He arrived hot-foot, all attired in his Sabbath best complete with top-hat, and sought an interview with the adjutant of the police.

"My name is Avigdor Green," he said. "I'm a lawyer of Plonsk, and I have come to request the release of my son, David. I promise to be responsible for his behaviour in the future."

The adjutant stared at him. "What a coincidence," he answered. "My name happens to be Green too—Victor Green." He told his Jewish visitor to take his son home, and not allow him to get into mischief in Warsaw again. Thankfully, Avigdor led the erring youth out of the prison gates.

David had much to tell his friends of Ezra on his return to Plonsk: his days under lock and key, the treatment he received, the important people he had met at the Zionist gatherings, the way of life in the big city. He himself had but one question, which was burning on his lips. "What news of Herzl?" he wanted to know.

"His condition is serious," they told him. "People are saying he will not live very long."

This was true. Although still a young man in his early forties, Herzl was worn out. Daily bulletins about his condition were received, and each was more grave than the last.

In the early summer of 1904, David Green with his closest friends, Shlomo Zemach and Shmuel Fuchs, went off on a holiday. There they heard the worst. Theodor Herzl, the Jew who had risen less than ten years before to give his people new hope, who had been their spokesman before kings and emperors, was dead.

What would happen to their dreams now? None could say. All they knew was that a long time must elapse before a leader of his quality would arise again.

The trio of friends returned home, each with his separate dreams. During the next few months many changes occurred in their lives. Shmuel Fuchs left to join relatives in America. The others were never to see him again. David carried on with his work for Poale Zion. He travelled up and down the country, rousing the younger Jews to a new sense of purpose.

Shlomo Zemach had a plan of his own. His parents were rich. They wanted him to enrol at one of the great European universities, such as Vienna or Berlin. But his thoughts lay elsewhere, among the vineyards of Palestine, where he knew some of his people were already working. One night he took 300 roubles from his father's cash-box, left a farewell note, and disappeared. In the space of a few weeks he was in Jaffa, and writing a letter home imploring his father's forgiveness.

David's work kept him in Poland. But he knew it could not be for long. Zionism meant for him, too, a life of daily toil in the country he already knew so well from his reading. He would be a labourer also. He would join Shlomo in the vineyards. He would live on bread and olives and help to build up a home for the Jews to give them a place among nations.

Palestine called to him, and soon he would come.

CHAPTER TWO

New Life in an Ancient Land

SHLOMO ZEMACH wrote many letters to David about his life in Palestine. They made him dream more and more about going there himself, even though there would be many difficulties in his way. It simply did not seem right to him that, while he went about making speeches and attending meetings on Zionism, his friend and many others like him were already working on the land, exerting every muscle of their bodies to smooth the path for those who would follow.

One summer's day in 1905, a knock at the door of his father's house in Plonsk brought David Green a most welcome if unexpected visitor. It was Shlomo. The young pioneer had returned home for a visit. He had been worried all this time by the guilty way he had left his parents the year before, and he wanted them to forgive him.

Of course, Shlomo was forgiven! Of course, everyone in Plonsk was happy to see him, and to hear from his own lips about his way of life! They fired a thousand questions at him: "How many Jews worked on the land in Palestine?" "How many lived in the towns, and what did they do for their livelihood?" "Were their Turkish rulers cruel?" "Did their Arab neighbours welcome the Jews?"

Shlomo tried to give answers to all these questions, and to many more. Gradually, the people of Plonsk were able to piece together a picture of daily life in the Holy Land. It was not altogether a happy picture. The story unfolded by the earnest youth, his face bronzed by the hot Asian sun, was of hardships, and many disappointments. This was especially the case among those who came to the country with little money or, as often happened, with none at all.

They begged him to explain. "I am sorry to say that the Jewish farmers do not welcome us when we come to them for work," Shlomo told them. "They are used to employing Arabs, who will work for much less pay than we do, as they need so much less."

"Then is work *nowhere* to be found?"

"Not exactly. There are some friendly Jewish farmers, but they are just a handful. Only in the great wine-presses can we find employment easily, at Zichron Yaacov and Rishon le Zion." They understood that the reason for this was the Jewish law that no Gentile could have a hand in making the wine, otherwise it would not be kosher.

The visitor described the remote Jewish villages high up in the north of the country, in the region of Galilee. There, the pioneers were finding things very tough indeed. They were cut off from their fellow-Jews who kept together in the southern colonies around Jaffa. They lived in the heart of the wildest part of the country, were often stricken by fever and were far from their friends. Marshland, where disease bred, was all around them, but the soil they actually tilled was hard and stony.

David Green drank in every word Shlomo spoke, particularly his description of Galilee. He was spell-bound by it, and could not get the idea out of his mind that, when he should at last find himself in Palestine, it was in distant Galilee that he would make his home.

As they wandered over their old haunts together David and his friend spent much time discussing politics. Shlomo's ideas had changed. He thought it was wrong to worry too much about Socialism. That was all very well for the Jews in Europe, but their job was to get young people to come to Palestine, in larger and larger numbers, and forget all else for the time being. The only thing their people should be taught was the need to work on the land, so that the Jews could become farming folk as in the days of the Bible.

David did not take this view. "We can't throw away all we have built up," he argued fiercely. "You have suffered so much in Palestine because your workers did not band together and so could not help each other. There are more workers than employers. They *must* be strong, or they will lose heart."

He spoke with passion. David believed that every Jew in Palestine should help the cause of Zionism, not make profits out of the weakness of his fellow-Jew.

Shlomo shook his head doubtfully. "When you

come to Palestine, you will worry about earning your daily bread, and how to get used to the climate, and what language you will speak. All these things come before politics."

"They are all part of politics," David retorted. Perhaps they were both right. At all events, the friends could not reach agreement on the question.

The weeks wore on. Shlomo began to make his preparations to depart again, and this made David restless, and keen himself to be on his way. One day he blurted out to his father: "I'm going with Shlomo. We'll be travelling to Palestine together."

Avigdor was not altogether happy about this news. He had known, of course, that his son intended to become one of the pioneers, but somehow could not face the idea of their separation. It might be for ever.

"You ought to stay with us a little longer, David," he objected. "At least until you have finished your studies."

"Poland has no more to offer me," replied the son. "You are a Zionist too, Father. I know you'll agree to my plan in the end."

Avigdor turned to his trusted old friend, Rabbi Simcha Isaac, for support. But he received none from that quarter.

"The lad is right," declared the rabbi, with a vigorous shake of his wise old head. "The future of all of us lies in Eretz Israel. And what's more, I'm going, too!"

This ended all argument. If a man of 50 could embark on such an adventure, how could Avigdor stand in the way of a youth of 19? But his eyes were misty with tears as he gave the plan his blessing.

As a matter of fact, the kind of discussion that had been going on between Avigdor Green and his son David was having its echo in many other Plonsk families. Rabbi Simcha and young Green were not the only two who planned to return with Shlomo Zemach. There were at least a dozen others, and not only young people. Some of the parents themselves were busy packing their bags, too, until that day in September, 1906, when after much feasting, dancing and speech-making (in which Reb Avigdor of course took a prominent part) the happy band started on their long and adventurous journey to the land of their dreams, hardly thinking of the difficulties and hardships that lay ahead.

The first halting-place on their journey was the Russian port of Odessa, on the Black Sea. They reached it after many hours on the train. Here David and his friend Shlomo sought an interview with a famous Zionist leader named Menahem Ussishkin. They wanted to explain how they proposed to bring the Jewish youth of Eastern Europe to join them in a life of toil in building up the homeland.

David was ambitious. His idea was to found a newspaper with the object of informing those yet to come of all that working in Palestine meant. But printing a newspaper, and then sending it out across the world, required money. He and Shlomo had no doubt, as they trudged up the stairs of the old building which housed the Zionist offices, that Ussishkin would give it to them. In this, however, they were doomed to disappointment.

"We are not yet ready to invite young people to Palestine," the leader told them. "After all, we have only just started our political work. We have not yet had the approval of the Turkish Government. We have to send doctors out there first, and experts in farming to prepare the way." For some reason, he seemed rather angry with the two young men for daring to make up their own minds about going to Palestine without first being asked.

"Do you want to die of malaria?" he almost shouted.

No, they did not want to die. But what was the purpose in waiting? Everyone kept telling them to wait. They were ready to give themselves whole-heartedly to the land which was in all their thoughts and prayers. With the right spirit and determination there was nothing they could not achieve.

"All right, go if you must," said Ussishkin, after he had heard their protests. "But we here have no money for your newspaper. We send out magazines of our own. Send me your articles and I shall see to it that they are printed."

This was not what they were after, and the two friends left Ussishkin without accepting his grudging offer. Somewhat downcast, they went into the street, only to be confronted by the cheerful, ruddy face of a man who looked the very opposite of a city gentle-man.

"And where are you two young fellows off to?" he asked them, in Russian.

"We're on our way to Eretz Israel," they replied, "though"—pointing a scornful finger towards the office they had just quitted—"nobody seems to want us to go."

"Nonsense! Of course you're wanted. We need the help of strong young hands. I have a farm in Petach Tikva, just a few miles from Jaffa. Be sure to come and see me there."

They looked gratefully at the stranger. As it happened, they were planning to make Petach Tikva their first stopping-place in Palestine. This was more in the spirit they had expected. And they continued on their journey in a more hopeful frame of mind.

A short sea journey through the Dardanelles and the small ship that carried the group from Plonsk steamed into Jaffa harbour. This Mediterranean port was of far more importance in those days than it is now. For it was the chief means of entry into Palestine from the West, and almost as busy as the Egyptian port of Alexandria, where ships docked for passengers who wished to travel overland into the Holy Land by way of the Sinai desert. It must be remembered that Haifa had not yet been built, while the aeroplane, of course, was little more than an inventor's dream.

Jaffa was a most colourful little port. Within it dwelt people of various nationalities, all in the dress of their native countries. There were many rich traders, Turkish, French or English; Armenian shop-keepers; Arab guides or beggars; missionaries and monks; and an office set up by the Zionist Organisation. There were also several inns quite near the dockside, two of which were kept by Jews for their own people as they disembarked.

David and his party were really illegal immigrants. They had no official permission to land, for the Turkish Government which ruled Palestine at that time was opposed to the Jews' coming. Most of those already in the country were either Turkish citizens or citizens of some other country, and had made proper arrangements in advance for settling in Palestine. But a little matter like official permission did not daunt the Zionist pioneers.

They overcame the obstacle by paying a small bribe to the Customs Officer. This was a regular practice at Jaffa, and the business was done quietly and without fuss by officials of the Zionist Organisation. The group from Plonsk, and a few other Jews who had joined them along their route, were therefore allowed to land and to make their way to one or other of the Jewish inns.

This was a moment the humble young man, as he clutched his bundle of possessions and walked along the cobbled streets, was never to forget. He was here, in Palestine, the land of the Bible! This was the country he was to help turn into the homeland of his people, as it had been thousands of years before! This was the scorching sunlight that his eyes must learn to bear, after the long, cold winters of Eastern Europe. This was the language (he heard much Arabic) that he must master. Inwardly, he made a pledge to put his love for this country above everything else. He would live for it, and labour for it, so that the Jew might stand up to his fellow-man in pride and strength, and be his equal.

David's spirit soared on the wings of these thoughts,

but his body was heavy with the need to rest. As a member of Poale Zion, there was a welcome awaiting him at one of the modest houses that served as an inn for workers like himself, and he sat down to eat heartily and make his plans.

He was not to be left alone for long. There were some people at the inn who had arrived in Palestine a year or two before, and one by one they came up to the stranger and exchanged news with him. David, on his part, was anxious to hear of their experiences, for they were 'old hands'.

Some of those with whom he talked were full of enthusiasm for their new life; others were in drooping spirits. It was just as Shlomo had said. The work, when they found it, was hard; one had to get used to the climate. It was soon made plain to David that for every person who was grateful for the chance to prove himself in the country, there was another looking for a ship to take him back to Europe. There were optimists and pessimists. Some thought he was mad to have come; others praised him for taking the plunge.

It was to the latter that David Green addressed himself.

"Tell me about Petach Tikva," he begged them. "My friend Zemach and I will be going there to-morrow to look for work."

Petach Tikva, they informed him, was a few miles inland. It was a township in its beginnings. A dozen farmsteads were occupied by Jewish colonists, mostly from Russia, who had settled there ten or twenty years before. A rich French Jew, Baron Edmond de

Rothschild, had helped them to start their farms, and as a result they were now fairly well-established. These colonists were on quite friendly terms with their Arab neighbours, many of whom they employed.

"So far, so good," thought David Green. And he slept contentedly through the night. The next day, after two hours walk along rough roads and across sandy plains, he and Shlomo found themselves in Petach Tikva. They looked for the friendly man they had met in Odessa. They found him, and their luck held good. For he greeted them warmly and took them along to one of his neighbours, and this farmer engaged them both to work in his fields. For wages they received just enough to rent an attic-room in the village, and to buy one decent meal a day.

David, delighted with his fortune, wrote home to his father: "My dream has became a reality. I'm so happy. There is the rich smell of cornfields, the braying of donkeys, the leaves rustling in the orchards. I'm in Eretz Israel."

During the busy days that followed, as David's hands roughened in the long hours of toil, he constantly asked himself: "Is this all that I am to do here? I have become a worker, and am helping to re-build our homeland. But does Zionism ask no more of me?" And he answered his own thoughts: "No, I must get all the workers to band together, so that they become stronger than their masters, and make this homeland the place where the Jewish worker will have justice."

It was these ideas which prompted him, and many

others, to attend a conference in Jaffa. This was the first conference of the Poale Zion party ever to be held in Palestine. What a strange assortment of young men and women they looked, the forty or so who turned up to discuss their future, and the country's future! For the most part they wore the heavy European garments that they had brought with them, but in some way adapted to the climate of Palestine. The men had all manner of head-gear to protect them from the sun: broad-brimmed, 'ten-gallon' hats, like Texas cowboys; a 'boater' or two, favoured in those days by the smart young fellows of Edwardian London, and the working-man's cloth cap. Some strode proudly along in the flowing Arab *keffiya*, purchased, no doubt, for a few piastres from a native acquaintance. Their shirts were generally of the Russian *rubaschka* type—tight round the neck but worn loose over the trousers.

Their clothes might have varied considerably, but not their ideas. All of them were concerned with one problem: how to turn themselves into a nation, or at least a centre out of which a nation could grow. They knew that they needed to speak one language—Hebrew. Also, they had to get the idea accepted that Jews had to work on the land; and, most important of all, they must attract thousands of young people from abroad to their ranks.

David Green was shocked to discover that a good half of those present could not speak Hebrew. He begged his comrades to abandon Yiddish, their European language, in their new life.

"Yiddish is the language of the ghetto," he told

them. "It belongs to the bad old days of our persecution and shame in Europe." The rebirth of their
people, he went on, depended as much upon the
revival of their ancient Biblical tongue as upon
settlement and self-labour. Whoever heard of a
nation without a national language! But Yiddish
belonged to their exile.

This was quite a speech, and it made all the others
sit up and take notice. Who was this newcomer from
the little Polish town few of them had ever heard
of, and with the blisters still on his palms through
lack of experience with pick and shovel?

A few of his hearers laughed at David's ideas. They
knew, of course, that the Zionists were trying to
revive Hebrew, and that several scholars were writing books on the subject, and publishing newspapers.
But this had nothing to do with them.

"Do you expect us to go to school again?" one of
them called out to David.

"If Jews can't speak Hebrew, are we to turn them
away from Palestine?" shouted another.

"How can the language used in our prayers be
made to serve us in modern times?" was another
objection.

Of course, it seemed fantastic. But David stood his
ground. There would be no Jewish nation without
Hebrew, he answered, angry at being the centre of
a dispute.

Even those who disagreed with his views admired
David for the way he conducted his argument. He
gave them heart. And by the time the conference
was over, and they went their separate ways again,

B

they accepted David Green as one of their leaders.

He had begun to climb the Poale Zion ladder. Important tasks were now given to him. His comrades asked him to be their spokesman in the quarrels that cropped up with their employers. He helped new arrivals, from the moment they stepped off the boat until they were settled in work and lodgings. He worked out plans for getting the Poale Zion members respected by the Zionist leaders in Europe.

David even managed to start his newspaper. But this, to his disappointment, had to be published in Yiddish. It was hand-written and copied, then went the rounds of the colonies. Three issues only were produced because he and his friends decided after this that it would be better to wait until they could get something out in printed form.

He loved the work in the fields, even though it tired him at first. His job meant arduous toil from dawn to dark, planting corn and vegetables, tending the mules, sometimes guiding the plough along the furrows, behind a team of oxen or a camel. At times he was laid low by sickness or exhaustion, but his tough young body soon got well again. In the evenings there was a cool breeze to shake off his tiredness, and David and Shlomo would meet their friends at a little café, there to sing lustily the songs they remembered from their old homes, refreshed by endless cups of sweet Turkish coffee.

Neither David nor Shlomo intended to stay in Petach Tikva for long. They ached to travel the country, and to try their luck up north. Shlomo had already been up there. Now he was off again, and as the friends separated they vowed to meet later in some new area that the Jews intended to open up by the labour of their own hands.

Shortly after Shlomo's departure, the Petach Tikva farmers bought some more land at Kfar Saba, seven miles up country. A local Arab chieftain sold it to them, but warned them that his Pasha would not allow them to build houses there, except on payment of a large sum of money.

Nevertheless, David went up to Kfar Saba. He found work at once, because the farmers, who only came to look over their property occasionally, knew that the Jewish labourers, unlike the Arabs, would work whether they were watched or not.

When Avigdor Green opened the next letter from his son he read: "The air here is clear and healthy, because we are situated on a hill and are surrounded by mountains. We start at six in the morning, and as the sun rises high the sweat pours from us like a river." It was a happy letter, but nevertheless Avigdor was worried about his son. Those anxieties increased during the coming months as, walking along the narrow streets of Plonsk, he met some of those who had left for Palestine with David that September day in 1906, but had now returned.

"Why have you come back?" he asked them.

They replied with a chorus of complaints: "I was sick with malaria, it was hopeless trying to go on. . . ." "I was hungry. We didn't earn enough to buy a square meal. . . ." "I was homesick. . . ." "You think Palestine is a land of milk and honey! We're not wanted there. Nobody will help us along. If we'd

35

stayed much longer we'd have died in the desert."

The old man went back home and wrote to his son, demanding to know why so many people painted the country in such black colours. David's reply came almost by return of post.

"The new Jew is full of fight," he wrote. "He won't go back to the old life!" And scornfully he went on: "Zionism is a struggle, and I can only feel sorry for those who have fled the battlefield, and in their cowardice blame conditions here. Haven't I told you, Father, of our troubles? The people you've been meeting wouldn't climb out of the bog they live in even if they heard that the streets of Palestine were paved with gold!"

Some, indeed, did leave. But there were always more to replace them. And it was a happy day for David whenever he had business in Jaffa and saw there the fresh, pale faces of young idealists who had come to join in the work. One of them particularly aroused his interest, for he spoke Hebrew fluently, and seemed to know a great deal about politics.

David overheard the newcomer explain how, in the part of Russia where he used to live, the Poale Zion members had secret training in self-defence, such as shooting and ju-jitsu. They did this in order to protect themselves and their families during the pogroms. This gave David an idea.

"We might do something like that over here," he observed.

"Yes, I have often thought about it," said the stranger. "I was here three years ago, as a student, so I know something of your problems." The two talked on together, and discovered that their points of view were similar on many of the problems of building up the Jewish homeland.

"I'm David Green, of Plonsk," said David at length, extending his hand.

"I'm Isaac Ben-Zvi, of Poltava," said the other.

So it was that a long and fruitful friendship began. Their partnership lasted over fifty years, through hard times and good, and long after the one had become Prime Minister of the State of Israel and the other its President.

CHAPTER THREE

The Worker Takes a Rifle

YOUNG people who feel they are doing important work sometimes grow impatient with the
slowness and caution of their elders. The Jewish
pioneers on the land were certainly no exception.
Frankly, they were 'fed up' with the men who had
taken over the leadership of Zionism after Herzl's
death in 1904. True, the Congress met regularly in
European cities, but it seemed to do little else but
talk. And, the young men of Petach Tikva and Rishon
le Zion and Kfar Saba and Galilee thought, their
talk had little connection with reality.

Somehow the fire seemed to have gone out of the
Zionist movement. It lacked the drive and spirit of
Herzl's leadership.

What could they do about this? The old farmers
who felt they were so generous in giving them work
might rest on their laurels if they liked. Let them
carry on with their cheap Arab labour in their small-
holdings, but that was not Jewish pioneering. There
had been Jewish farmers before them in Poland and
Russia and Rumania, also employing Gentile peasants.

This was not good enough for Poale Zion. Its members saw no reason why they should not move forward on their own.

Indeed, why should not the Zionist leaders buy land for the workers to develop, extending the Jewish holdings outward from the existing 'pockets' in various parts of the country? The Jewish National Fund had been created some years before for this very purpose. Why should it not give small plots of land to the workers? Then the Jewish pioneers, working on the soil without the aid of Arab labourers, could really prove themselves.

So ran their thoughts, and Isaac Ben-Zvi was sent to Europe as the Poale Zion spokesman at the Zionist Congress. David Green, in the meantime, went up to Galilee, thus fulfilling a wish that had been with him since his early talks with Shlomo Zemach in Plonsk.

It was a perilous journey in those days, by foot most of the way across stretches of country infested with robber tribes. It took David two days to reach the village of Sejera, at the foot of Mount Tabor and between Nazareth and the Carmel mountain range. How primitive it all seemed to him, so that Judea was now a luxurious memory! And sure enough, over in the fields, David was soon able to pick out the bending form of Shlomo Zemach. They had been separated for more than a year.

As it happened, more than distance had divided them. Their ideas and opinions had also travelled farther and farther apart, as the friends were soon to discover.

Shlomo did not care for David's political views.

He was not against Socialism, he insisted, but he thought the time was not ripe to adopt such European ideas in Palestine. This was why he had joined another group which was growing up side-by-side with Poale Zion. It was called Hapoel Hatzair—the Hebrew for 'Working Youth'. But in one respect neither of the two had changed: they put their love for their country above all else.

David now spoke Arabic in addition to Hebrew, and in Sejera he was able to meet the Arabs and observe how they lived. He was curious to know what they thought about the Jews, who worked from dawn to dusk and then spent the evenings singing their strange songs. Sejera lay in the midst of rough country and the local tribes carried on their lives as they had done for centuries.

Sometimes these Arabs would swoop down from the hills and steal the Jews' oxen, or burn down a barn. This was a constant worry to the farmers, who used local native villagers as their watchmen. But none were completely trustworthy.

The truth of the matter was, these northern Arabs did not welcome the arrival of the Jews on their very doorstep, as it were. They regarded them as foreigners, with strange customs and the ability to work at a feverish pace. The Arab loved his leisure, and squatted for hours cross-legged in his coffee-house, while the Jew hastened hither and thither, building, building, building all the time. And in the coffee-houses, the Arabs mumbled and grumbled.

David and Shlomo worked for an old farmer named Abraham Roshavsky, in whose house they also shared a room. This white-bearded settler looked more like a rabbi than a countryman. He was a jovial soul, and kind to his workers.

"I've lived among the Arabs for years," the old man used to say. "They are my friends. They will be yours too when you grow to understand them."

David Green could not agree, but for a long time he kept his peace. It was all very well for farmer Roshavsky to talk like that. He would not be the one to go farther and farther afield, as more land was bought by the Jewish National Fund. It was the worker who would go out, alone for long hours, surrounded by hostile eyes, and clear the wild shrubs, drain the marsh or plant the seedlings.

Almost in a whisper he talked the problem over with Shlomo. For already secret moves were taking place, on the lines suggested by Ben-Zvi, for Jewish watchmen.

"We shall have to take over guard duty in Sejera," said David. "We shall have to carry arms, and I know this is risky. But there's no other way of keeping our possessions safe."

Shlomo shook his head. "We shall be making a mistake, David. We've come here as men of peace, and as the Arabs' friends. How can we expect them to welcome us if they see us carrying rifles?"

"We Jews dare not rely on others to defend us," David persisted, his eyes gleaming. "That was why we always suffered in the past. If we want to become a nation we must learn to look after ourselves."

"And that means dismissing the watchmen we now employ, who are a wild lot anyway."

41

B*

"We shall have to face it sooner or later," said David.

Down in Jaffa a group of Jewish volunteers, armed with rifles, were already guarding the farms. Now the Sejera workers did the same. They laboured by day, stood sentry by night. David Green was one of them.

Shlomo's warnings were only too soon realised. The dismissed guards, angered at the turn of events, now robbed the property they once protected. Sejera became a frontier-post for the Jews. Tension rose. Shots rang out in the night. David once went out to rescue a comrade mixed up in a shooting affray, only to bring him back dead.

The Arabs thought they could frighten the Jews into leaving the place. But the newcomers held on to Sejera. They were in Palestine to stay, and their neighbours must learn to accept them. If they gave up here, or for that matter anywhere else in their colonies, it would spell the end of their work everywhere.

The Sejera group were so much respected throughout the colonies for their pioneering skill and bravery that they were given a new task to help carry the Zionist work forward. David Green called a meeting of his comrades one day because, he said, the head of the Jaffa office had a special proposal for them to discuss. This man's name was Dr. Ruppin, and he told them about a new stretch of land just bought beside the River Jordan. He wanted a dozen young men and women to go there and clear the area, then settle there permanently. He would see that they received enough money to keep them going until they could support themselves from their own crops.

Yes, they would do it, they said. The Arab name

for the piece of land was Um-Juni. When they arrived there they renamed it Daganya. They decided to work it together, sharing everything, for they took this as an opportunity to practise Socialism as well as preach it. And hidden well from sight in the baggage cart they pulled towards their new land was a pile of rifles and ammunition.

At Daganya no one would take more money than he needed. No one had more clothes than his neighbour. They ate together in a crude wooden shack that was a dining-hall and meeting-place and children's nursery. As they prospered, they had more to share, and took in more people. The Hebrew language was scrutinised for a special word for this type of communal village. And they found the word 'kibbutz'.

David had other work in Galilee, and did not accompany his comrades. But as they moved away, it seemed to the young Poale Zion leader that they had made another step forward in forming the pattern of the new Jewish nation : the Hebrew language was gaining ground; the Jewish worker was showing the way to conquering the deserts and marshes of Palestine with his own labour, not the labour of others; and self-defence, too, was accepted as being the sole means by which they could protect what they built.

As for Shlomo Zemach, he decided at this point to separate from his friend and, leaving Sejera behind, he moved even farther north, to Rosh Pina. There some Rumanian Jews had begun to farm a stretch of land on a hill-side. Shlomo had instructions from his own Hapoel Hatzair to persuade them to accept Jewish workers.

It was 1908, and David had been in the country barely two years. How it was changing already! More workers arrived in Galilee, from Poland and Russia and the Baltic countries, even from England and France. He travelled among them, and told them that, no matter what part of the world they came from, they were all Jews and must learn to live together in harmony.

Then, in distant Constantinople, there took place an event which was to change his entire life. Tired of the Sultan's misrule, some young officers seized power. They formed a Government and promised freedom to all the peoples within the Turkish Empire.

David was summoned by Poale Zion to Jerusalem. He was given the task, together with Isaac Ben-Zvi and a young girl named Rachel Yanait, to produce a regular Hebrew newspaper. For the Poale Zion leaders assumed that the announcement from Constantinople referred to the Jews, who also were a people within the Turkish Empire. They wanted freedom, too, and, through their newspaper, they would work for it.

The first issue came out in 1910. In it was a long political article about the place of the Palestinian worker in the Zionist movement. At the bottom there was a signature never before seen in print. It was "Ben-Gurion".

David Green no longer existed. The boy had become a man. The Hebrew name by which he now described himself would one day be familiar to people the world over.

CHAPTER FOUR

"Leave This Country, Never to Return!"

WHEREVER David travelled in Palestine, he was reminded of his Bible. He knew the history of every hillock and township, even the smallest rivulet. The stories told in the Book of Joshua and in the writings of the Prophets came alive before his eyes.

He therefore thought it a great privilege to live in Jerusalem, the Holy City, and to work with such a noble soul as Ben-Zvi. Of course, he regretted deeply having to change his open-air way of life, but this was more than compensated for when he wandered through the ancient streets of the city which has inspired human beings for more than two thousand years, and has been the focus of Jewish longing throughout the ages.

The man who was now known as Ben-Gurion set up his modest office above a little shop in an outlying district called Zichron Moshe. This district was named after a great English Jew, Moses Montefiore, who had given vast sums to build a housing quarter outside the old city walls. Out of this quarter was later to grow the New City of Jerusalem.

It was exciting to produce that newspaper. The three editors, Ben-Gurion, Ben-Zvi and Rachel Yanait, thoroughly enjoyed writing the articles and then watching the bearded old printer set them up in neat rows of type. They poured heart and soul into their words, and found eager readers all over the country.

After a few issues *Ha'achdut*, as it was called (the word means 'unity') became so popular that they brought it out weekly instead of monthly. In its columns Ben-Gurion often discussed the changes that were taking place in Constantinople. He urged the Jews to hasten their demands for equality with the other subject peoples of the Turkish Empire, such as the Arabs, Bulgars, Slovenes and Kurds. Especially should the Jews have the right to enter Palestine freely, without the tiresome and costly tricks of bribery that were now necessary.

Furthermore, they were entitled to the right of running their own affairs within Palestine. After all, no less than 130,000 Jews lived in the country in the year that *Unity* first made its appearance, 1910. Small groups of people of the same race within a country are known as 'minorities'. Well, the Jews too were a minority and had problems all their own which only they could solve.

Soon the old impatience attacked Ben-Gurion's spirit. The new rulers in Constantinople were moving too slowly for his liking. And as he talked the problem over with Ben-Zvi, he wracked his brain for a way to press their views in the right places, and to reach the topmost councils of the Empire. It could not be done merely by writing articles.

Suddenly the two hit upon a plan. If Constantinople was the capital of the Empire, why should they not go there in person, to learn what they could about the system of government there, make themselves known as spokesmen of the Jewish minority in Palestine, and perhaps form important friendships with leading officials? If they learned to speak the Turkish language, and a proper Parliament was set up in the capital, was there not a chance that they might be elected Jewish members of that Parliament?

A bold plan? Of course it was. But the whole idea of Jewish rebirth as a nation was bold. Then Ben-Gurion and Ben-Zvi received news that the Zionist leaders in Europe were themselves looking hopefully in the direction of Constantinople. They had gone so far as to establish an office there, with Vladimir Jabotinsky, a Russian Zionist who was later to win fame in the movement, in charge.

This settled it. Poale Zion had no intention of lagging behind. And thus it was that when term began at Constantinople University in the autumn of 1912, two new law-students were enrolled: David Ben-Gurion and Isaac Ben-Zvi, each with a brand-new fez on his head. Later they were joined by other comrades. Among them was Moshe Shertok, a brilliant youth whom fortune was also to lead to great heights in after years.

As had so often happened before, the young friends were bitterly disappointed in what they saw of Constantinople, and equally dismayed by the coldness with which they were received at the Zionist headquarters there. The Turkish revolution proved in fact to be quite different from what Ben-Gurion imagined it to be from the reports he had had in Jerusalem. He looked in vain for the freedom and justice that were supposed to replace corruption, poverty and intrigue. He was moved to anger by the wickedness he saw openly practised among both the highest and the most humble. And when the young comrades approached the Zionist officials, to volunteer their help in the important work that had to be done, their offer was spurned.

"You get on with your studies," they were advised. "Politics are not your business." How wrong their elders were!

Nevertheless, they did plunge into their work at the University. David began a course in Constitutional Law, and found this a study of absorbing interest, for it gave him an insight into the workings of the Turkish system of controlling the sprawling Empire. In fact he became so engrossed in it that he began to wonder whether he would ever again be a labourer in the fields.

He wrote to his father about this. "I shall have to make up my mind pretty soon whether to remain a farm-worker or become a lawyer," his letter said. "I have no doubt that I would be happy in either occupation. In making a choice, the only question in my mind will be to decide which would be more for the good of the land of Israel. That is my sole concern."

Avigdor, who was a lawyer himself, did not write a detailed reply to his son. Instead, he sent him enough money to help him live in Constantinople and complete his university course. It was the old man's way of showing that he approved of his son's following in his own footsteps.

The outcome of Ben-Gurion's studies took the form of a book, which was published in Hebrew. It explained the legal basis of the various Provinces of the Empire, and their relationship to the central Government in Constantinople. The information it contained showed clearly that Turkey was a weak Power, and able to control the affairs of the Empire only with the greatest difficulty.

At the University, there was a general feeling of trouble in the air. Visitors poured into Constantinople from all the capitals of the world, and each brought tidings to show that the clouds of war were gathering fast in Europe. Yet the students from Palestine thought they should remain in Turkey as long as possible. They clung to the belief that the Empire's leaders would keep their promises, and therefore they should be at hand to influence the course of events. As they travelled around the city they looked exactly like young Moslem noblemen reared to cherish the Koran rather than the Bible.

Alas, the tragedy that everybody feared burst upon an unhappy world in August, 1914. Britain, France and Russia were at war with Germany and Austria. Soon other countries came in, and pacts of alliance between various countries began to take effect. Germany was joined by Bulgaria, then by Turkey. It seemed as though all Europe was going up in flames.

What of the position of the Jews in all these countries? They had to answer the call to the colours no matter where they lived. This meant they had to fight their fellow-Jews, even though their feelings about the conflict were far from clear. They hated Russia because of the cruelties perpetrated against them; yet many found themselves sharing her cause. Others, who lived in various parts of the Turkish Empire, had to defend what they as yet had no reason to trust. German Zionists confronted British and French Zionists in the grim battles in Northern France.

As for the Jews living in Palestine, they were trapped. Turkey poured soldiers into the country, but would only put those Jews into uniform who were her citizens. The British were in Egypt, planning an invasion of Palestine and the Turkish Provinces farther north and east. In this confused and desperate situation, Ben-Gurion and Ben-Zvi decided that they must go back to their people.

After a difficult journey they eventually reached Jerusalem. Here they discovered that many Jews, especially those who had entered the country illegally, had fled. The settlers in Judea were driven northward, into Galilee. Husbands and wives were sent in different directions. The Zionists were looked upon as enemies in league with the Allied Powers. The patient work of years was destroyed overnight, and it seemed plain to all that those Jews engaged in politics had better make themselves scarce. The two students wondered what their next move should be.

Their next move was—to prison. Soon after they got back, Ben-Gurion and Ben-Zvi went over to their newspaper office. The police swooped down on them there, took away all the documents they could find, arrested the two students who, a few weeks earlier, had hoped to be accepted for the Turkish Army, and sent them to jail.

The Turks felt they had good grounds for keeping the Poale Zion comrades under lock and key. They knew that the Zionist leaders of England and France, led by Chaim Weizmann, were pressing the Allied Powers to support them in making Palestine into a Jewish homeland, offering in return Jewish help in the war. Consequently the Turks proposed to root the movement out of Palestine lest it become a 'fifth column' behind the lines.

Ben-Gurion was brought before a Turkish officer named Hassan Bey for interrogation.

"When did you become a Zionist?" he was asked.

"I was a Zionist in Russia, before coming to this country."

"Is it true that you recently attended a Zionist Congress in Vienna?"

"Yes."

"Who elected you a delegate to that Congress?"

"My friends in America."

This reply struck the questioner, not surprisingly, as being a falsehood. He could not be expected to know the complicated system by which delegates to Zionist Congresses were elected.

"According to my information," he persisted, "you were elected in Constantinople."

"No. I travelled from Constantinople. I was elected in America."

Hassan Bey pressed Ben-Gurion for details of Poale Zion members in Palestine, who they were, where they worked, where they came from. He was obviously trying to find out all he could about the Jewish self-defence organisation, which, of course, was against the law.

"Who are the leaders of your movement in Jerusalem?"

"I am."

"And who else?"

"My friend Ben-Zvi."

"And who else?"

"I know him, and I know myself."

In a fury, Hassan Bey yelled to the guard: "Take this dog back to jail, and bring the other one in."

But Ben-Zvi was not talking either. After a while, he too was led back to his cell.

As it happened, the Turks had done their spying over the years pretty thoroughly. There was little they did not know about the Zionists' activities, including the formation of a corps of armed guards for the colonies and the links which the movement was forging in Allied circles.

The two friends received a curt order a few days later. It was signed by Jamal Pasha, the Governor, himself. "Leave this country, and return only on pain of death!" it said.

This was worse even than they had feared. Was it possible that they would never see their beloved land again? As soon as the thought came into their minds they dismissed it. The war would not last for ever. The Jews had lived through many wars.

Nothing could crush their longing for Palestine.

They were given time to settle their affairs and, hanging on for as long as they could, they arranged for their work to be kept going in Palestine as far as possible. It was left in good hands, with young Jews who were Turkish citizens but not old enough for military service. They were instructed to pass on their orders to others should they in turn have to leave.

Moshe Shertok was among those deputed to carry on the secret work. Then, when his time came to join the Army, he left his instructions with his dearest friends, Eliahu Golomb and Dov Hos.

Only a few years before these three had been at school together, at the first Jewish High School in Palestine, called the Herzlia. How times had changed! When they were sitting at their desks, the school stood alone on a sand-dune to the north of Jaffa. Soon, houses and shops sprung up around it. In a little while this tiny Jewish suburb grew into a township. Its name was Tel Aviv.

Now, as they went their separate ways, they wondered whether Tel Aviv would still be there when the war ended. Or would their school, the houses and Jewry's hopes for a new homeland lay buried in the sand?

Rachel Yanait, the sole woman member of *Unity's* editorial staff, also remained behind. As she saw her comrades go off into exile, first Ben-Gurion and Ben-Zvi, then the others, she could barely stem the tears. But, like them, she refused to accept defeat. Perhaps the fulfilment of their aims would have to await the end of the war. Perhaps some of them would not live to see the outcome. Certainly times were going to be difficult in Palestine. There would be danger, and there would be hunger. But they would not despair.

CHAPTER FIVE

From the Old World to the New

EUROPE was a battlefield. There was only one country that the two Poale Zion leaders could enter without difficulty and where they would be able to go forward with their Zionist plans: the United States of America.

America was still neutral, and maintained friendly relations with Turkey. For many years before the first World War its gates had been open to millions of European immigrants, a large number of whom were Jews coming from the lands in the domain of the Czar of Russia. With the outbreak of war, and until America came into the struggle on the side of the Allies, this Jewish community grew enormously in importance, for it could keep in touch with the European Jews on both sides of the firing-line.

As for America as a whole, she had not yet achieved a position of world leadership, but the desire to help poorer countries than herself was already strong. Both Jews and non-Jews sent food and money to their relatives across the seas. Ships were chartered to carry urgent supplies wherever they were needed to aid innocent people.

David Ben-Gurion and Isaac Ben-Zvi, bound for New York, reached the Egyptian port of Alexandria in April, 1915, and shortly afterwards boarded ship to take them across the Atlantic. They could not look to the future with great confidence. In the first place, they knew no English, and they were almost penniless. Furthermore, their beliefs and ambitions led them eastward rather than to the west, to the Ancient World rather than to the New.

But they knew that a country which had welcomed millions of other Jews would find a place for them too; and as a result of their long experience in Poale Zion they were familiar, by name at least, with the party's leaders in New York and the other chief cities of America.

This was the task they set themselves: to enrol young men and women into the ranks of Zionism by persuading them to learn farming so that they might go to Palestine when the war ended. In addition to this, they intended to utilise their stay by spreading the idea of Jewish Socialism in Palestine.

For Ben-Gurion, it meant of course speaking the Yiddish of his childhood days. He and Ben-Zvi, together with other exiles from Palestine, toured the length and breadth of the great country to win people to their cause. They wrote articles, made speeches, organised branches of Poale Zion in dozens of towns.

They were appalled by the ignorance they found of what was happening in the Holy Land. Jewish boys and girls had been dying in the defence of the

colonies, yet here only a few knew about it. The two
exiles felt they owed a debt to those who had laid
down their lives in the defence of the Jewish homeland. They had to keep the memory of this heroism
alive. So they decided to write a book about the
Jewish colonies, and about those who had fallen in
the Zionist cause. It was a beautifully designed vol-
ume, written in Yiddish and entitled *Yiskor,* which
means "In Memoriam". It contained sketches and
drawings and was the kind of book the reader would
take down from his shelves again and again, and
wherever he dipped into the pages he would find
accounts of those early days, with their hardships
and triumphs.

Ben-Gurion wrote about Petach Tikva at the time
of his arrival there in 1906. He described his first days
in the fields, and how he gradually became a skilful
farm-worker. He told of the joy that came with till-
ing the soil of the Jewish homeland, and how it had
felt to take up the challenge of the plough.

This book was so successful that the authors
immediately began to write another. This was a reference work on the Holy Land, informing the reader
of the history of Palestine and its geography, and
about the various peoples who had inhabited it since
the Israelites were led into captivity by the Assyrians
hundreds of years before the Roman Empire.

In this way the year 1916 went its course. Ben-
Gurion's thoughts were as much in Europe as anywhere else, and he pored over the newspapers
eagerly for signs that the wearisome war would end.
But the rival armies seemed to be held in deadlock,

and the nations involved in the struggle looked, from America, as if they were bleeding to death.

Moreover, some very strange information was reaching him from London, and this did not exactly fit into his own plans. Ben-Gurion could not think of Palestine as being linked with any country except Turkey. He was still faithful to his old idea of giving the Jews a prominent voice in Turkish affairs. And he thought that his people should work for Turkey's victory in the war.

Others, however, had completely opposite views. In London the two most important leaders of the Zionist movement were Chaim Weizmann and Nahum Sokolow (neither of whom had even heard of Ben-Gurion at this time). And these two leaders looked to the British Government for support of the Zionist aims. In the course of their talks in London they let it be known that they would range the Jews of the world solidly behind England and France.

This turned everything into a sort of puzzle for Ben-Gurion, because he could not see how Turkey would receive them at the end of a war in which the Jews were the allies of her enemies.

The puzzle solved itself, however. In 1917, three great happenings occurred in quick succession: a revolution took place in Russia which swept away the Czar and his oppressive Government, and took that country out of the war; America came in on the side of the Allies, and prepared to send troops to the fighting-line; and Britain issued the famous Balfour Declaration, which gave its blessing to the Jewish longing to build a National Home in Palestine.

This was quite a lot for Ben-Gurion to digest. Any of these events alone would have required long hours of discussion with Ben-Zvi and other Poale Zion comrades on how it would effect their plans. Some things were obvious. The first was that, with America in the war, Germany and therefore Turkey stood much less chance of winning. The second was that, after the war, Britain rather than any other Power would have the most important say in Palestine's future.

They were exciting days—and nights—when the Poale Zion meetings were held in the upstairs rooms of cafés on New York's East-Side.

"Once more," Ben-Gurion told the others excitedly, "we can play our part, not just sit back as spectators."

"Yes," said Ben-Zvi, "we can continue where we left off, and with much greater chance of success."

"The world's greatest Empire is with us!"

"There'll be no more pogroms in Russia!"

Wherever Jews met together to talk, these two sentences were on their lips. People sang and danced in the streets of New York and Boston and Philadelphia, danced because America had at last made up her mind, and because it seemed as though a new dawn had begun for the Jewish people.

It was to Ben-Gurion and Ben-Zvi that the Jewish workers looked for guidance. These two were no longer just youthful pioneers. Life had turned them into wise politicians. They were still as idealist as ever they had been, but they were no longer content to leave important decisions for others to work out at the conference-table. Ben-Gurion was now thirty-one. He spoke as the representative of a nation, still spread over the four corners of the earth, perhaps, but nevertheless confident that it would soon be in possession of its homeland.

"We shall form a legion of volunteers within the British Army," he declared. "We shall fight to conquer Palestine alongside our allies. Then we shall fulfil the dream of Theodor Herzl, of returning to our land as free men."

He and his friends now started to work in America together with British agents to form a Jewish legion. They got into touch with Palestinian exiles all over the country, informing them of the decision. It was an exciting task. Over in Europe others, such as Jabotinsky (of the Constantinople office) and the one-armed Russian Zionist named Joseph Trumpeldor, were also engaged in it. Among the very first who volunteered were Ben-Gurion and Ben-Zvi, always ready to put into practice whatever they preached to others.

Still another event occurred that made Ben-Gurion wish ardently for the fulfilment of his plans. Soon after he joined the Army he became engaged to a girl he had frequently met at his meetings downtown, and at whose home he had been a welcome visitor. Her name was Paula Munweis, and she worked as a nurse at the Jewish hospital. Paula had been brought to America as a child from Minsk, in Russia. She had been a medical student, but her father had died suddenly and she had to give up her studies to help support her family.

Paula loved America, and it was not until she met David Ben-Gurion that she felt that Zionism was the way to solve Jewry's problems. It was a brave decision, to share the life of this very serious man, this restless messenger from Palestine who worked day and night for a country she had no great desire to see. Yet she agreed to become his wife, and follow him wherever destiny would take him, and accept the hardships as well as the joys of being a Jewish pioneer.

The man expelled from Palestine by the Turks, "never to return", left Nova Scotia in Canada after three months of military training and boarded a troopship to go to the Middle Eastern front. He was a private soldier in the 39th Battalion, the Royal Fusiliers. How proud he was of the Shield of David shoulder-flash on his uniform!

Yet the soldier never forgot that he was also a political leader, and this was understood also by those who were promoted to higher rank in the Army, but were junior to him in Zionist pioneering. For example, on his arrival in Egypt he met again his old Poale Zion comrade, Dov Hos, a sergeant-major now, but still a youth when Ben-Gurion had been expelled from Palestine. Rachel Yanait was in Egypt, too, doing welfare work for the British Army. She was now the fiancée, and would shortly be the bride, of Ben-Zvi.

Eagerly David asked for news from Palestine. The tidings brought by Rachel and Dov Hos filled him with grief. During the three years of his absence the Jews remaining in Palestine had suffered great distress. There had been a grave shortage of food and the Turks had herded them into camps to keep them from smuggling themselves over to the British lines.

Those pioneer settlements which had not been overrun in battle had fallen into decay through lack of workers. It was obvious they would have to start practically from the beginning again. In Palestine itself the fighting was now over. General Allenby, in command of the British troops, had entered Jerusalem even before Ben-Gurion's ship docked at Alexandria.

All this was bad enough, but what disgusted Ben-Gurion most was that he could not go to Jerusalem at once so as to pick up the threads again. The war was over as far as Palestine was concerned, yet when he asked to be discharged from the Army he was delayed for several months. Apparently, the British did not feel it wise to let these thousands of soldiers from America and other countries into Palestine all at once. They would not even allow them to do the normal occupation duties there, but rather kept them idle in Egypt. The British were obviously worried lest they displeased the Arabs with the sight of all these Jewish soldiers in the uniform of the victor.

At length, Ben-Gurion and his comrades-in-arms were demobilised, to find that many things were not working out as they expected. The British authorities did not seem to understand what the Jews were trying to do in Palestine, and Ben-Gurion did not think that Chaim Weizmann, the Zionist leader who was in the country with a host of important advisers, was very effective in teaching them.

Ben-Gurion saw now that a new struggle lay

ahead. They had the Balfour Declaration, and that meant that Jews could come into the country freely. They had Dr. Weizmann to speak for them at the Peace Conference, so that Jewish claims would be heard by all nations. But apart from this, Jerusalem seemed to him a half-dead city, and the Galilee colonies just ruins.

The workers, instead of getting on with the job of rebuilding, were split into all kinds of opposing groups and used their energies for the wrong purposes. Old familiar faces were absent, and the new ones which replaced them did not give him much heart. They did not know of the struggle to get Jewish labour into the colonies, they did not care about reviving the Hebrew language. And the British were not going to be as easy-going as the Turks when they discovered that some Jews had rifles and were an unofficial armed police-force.

It was, indeed, a despondent Ben-Gurion who hastened to Jaffa to greet his wife, Paula, when at long last she was able to reach the shores of Palestine. In her arms Paula proudly held the baby daughter he had not yet seen, and whom they had agreed to name Geula—the Hebrew word for 'redemption'.

CHAPTER SIX

Under the Union Jack

AFTER fluttering over vast stretches of the Middle Eastern regions of the world for more than four hundred years, the flag of Turkey was at last hauled down. The Sultan was no longer the overlord of the various countries of Arabia, he had lost his Balkan possessions, and his officials disappeared from the Holy Land. In fact, there was no such monarch as the Sultan any more. The defeated Turkey became a republic.

Palestine had a new master. In Jerusalem the Union Jack waved proudly against the blue skyline. The inhabitants of the country were subjects of King George V; and his representative, called the High Commissioner, was a Jew, Sir Herbert Samuel.

Britain did not rule Palestine as part of her Empire. She governed it on behalf of the League of Nations, holding what was known as a Mandate. This meant that Britain was to conduct the country's affairs until its own inhabitants were ready to do so for themselves.

It was not going to be an easy task. For Palestine

was holy to three great religions, Jewish, Christian and Moslem. For this reason millions of people in almost every country of the world were deeply interested in what happened in Palestine.

There were other complications. One of them was the promise contained in the Balfour Declaration to help the Jews build a National Home in Palestine although the Arabs were opposed to it. The latter took the view that the Jews had no right in the country at all.

The British felt, therefore, that they had to step very warily lest what they did for one section of the population would offend the other section, and *vice versa*. This did not mean that Britain did not want the job of governing Palestine. On the contrary. The Holy Land was desperately poor in resources, and at that time was mostly desert. But under the deserts of the neighbouring Middle Eastern lands that precious black liquid, oil, had been discovered—more than was known to exist in all the rest of the world together.

Palestine, with her long coastline, was an important link between that oil and its markets in Europe. Therefore, whoever controlled Palestine controlled a great deal besides. Britain was spending more money than any other Power to bring that oil to the surface, to refine it and funnel it through immense pipes hundreds of miles in length to the Mediterranean coast. Being the Mandatory Power in Palestine would place her in a convenient position to guard her investments.

For all these reasons, as well as for others, London

C

now comes very prominently into our story. Because Palestine was ruled from London, this city also became the most important Zionist centre. Dr. Weizmann set up his headquarters there, so as to keep in touch with the Government and to be on hand to advise it, if called upon.

No wonder, then, that one morning in 1920 David Ben-Gurion, together with his wife and baby daughter, stepped out of the shadows of Victoria Station and into a cab and disappeared in the stream of London traffic. He intended to make himself known in London, by British Zionist leaders as well as by British politicians. As a matter of fact, he was angry with both.

Ben-Gurion had just spent a year in one of the hardest but also one of the most important jobs of his life. He had helped to found a union of all the Jewish workers of Palestine. This union was called the Histadruth, which is the Hebrew word for 'organisation', and it dealt with many things besides wages and conditions of work. It founded schools and hospitals, built houses, started newspapers and even factories. The man from Plonsk was the Histadruth's General Secretary, which meant that he was the most powerful spokesman of the workers in Palestine.

His arrival in London went unnoticed. But it was not long before he made his presence felt. There was an important conference of Zionists going on in London at the time, and leaders of the movement from all parts of the world were there to discuss ways of raising large sums of money to buy land in

Palestine and begin reconstruction upon the ruins left by the war.

Into this busy conference scene stepped David Ben-Gurion. Dr. Weizmann sat in the President's chair.

"I have been sent by the workers of Palestine," said Ben-Gurion, his eyes flashing. "Because while you sit here talking they risk their lives building the National Home."

There were mutterings among the rows of delegates who heard him. "Who is this man, what does he want?" they asked each other.

"You have read that riots are breaking out in Palestine, that the Arabs are making trouble," he went on. "Do you know that those riots are costing the lives of our workers, both men and women, to whom Zionism means constant toil, disease, hunger? We need money to build houses, and to start new kibbutzim, but all we get are promises. We need the right to protect ourselves, but the British will not allow us to have arms. Yet they do not protect us with their own soldiers either. We cannot make the British understand our problems. They prefer to talk to you, in London, because they find you more patient and reasonable. Well," Ben-Gurion went on, "we cannot afford to be reasonable. Men who get malaria while draining marshes cannot be reasonable. The widows of the pioneers who die in Galilee cannot be reasonable."

"We are doing our best, what is it you want?" a delegate stormed back.

"We want to have more say in the affairs of the

Zionist movement," was the answer. "When the Turks ruled Palestine we used to go to them directly with our complaints. Now we have to do everything through you."

Dr. Weizmann, who greatly sympathised with the position of the workers, because he knew that the aims of Zionism could only be achieved slowly and with difficulty, explained the other point of view.

"We have had many promises of money to help in our work," he said. "But promises do not mean cash in the bank. We want to bring into Palestine all those thousands who are waiting to go there from Poland, Rumania and other countries. But we dare not do this unless we know we can feed them. At the moment we can only work with what we have. This means building up the country slowly, brick by brick, pioneer by pioneer, acre by acre."

"You do not stand up to the British," retorted Ben-Gurion. "They are obstructing our work."

"They will see things our way in the end, but it will take time. Let us be grateful for the help they have given us so far."

There was truth in both these arguments. Britain had given them the Balfour Declaration. But the Government would not be hurried. Neither did it read into that Declaration all that the Jews read into it. And the Zionists' greatest difficulty came from the fact that they had to buy every inch of land they colonised. They had to buy it from Arab landlords, and the more they wanted, the higher rose the price.

"We had to cover the soil of Palestine with Jewish gold," Weizmann afterwards wrote, in reply to critics like this 34-year-old representative of Poale Zion and Histadruth. "And for many, many years that gold came out of the pockets not of the Jewish millionaires, but of the poor."

Gold was hardly a subject about which Ben-Gurion could be termed an expert. He lived in a modest, two-roomed flat with his wife and daughter in a poor part of London, and he spent most of his time among the Jewish workers in the back streets of Whitechapel. There was a great deal that could be done without money, he thought. And he set out to do it.

Palestinian students were already coming to London to attend the University there, just as he and Ben-Zvi had gone to Constantinople. One of these was Moshe Shertok. Ben-Gurion saw his old comrade frequently, and together they worked out a plan to strengthen ties with the British Labour Party. There was only a handful of Labour Members in Parliament at that time, but Ben-Gurion was convinced that in a few years they would be strong enough to form the Government.

Then Ben-Gurion went off to the Continent, taking his family, now increased by the birth of a son, Amos, with him. He visited Paris, then Berlin, Prague, Vienna, Warsaw. He came to each city as the leader of the Palestine workers, and he addressed himself to the workers. And everywhere on his journey he secretly bought rifles and other small weapons, to be sent home to the settlements.

Almost at every stopping-place it seemed that he was met with bad news about some of his dearest friends. When he came to Vienna he read in the newspapers that Joseph Trumpeldor, the gallant one-armed pioneer, had been killed by Arabs while heroically defending a settlement in the far north of Palestine. Six comrades had died with him.

The Ben-Gurion family were in Plonsk, at the home of Avigdor Green, when David received a letter that made his heart heavy with sadness.

"What is it?" asked his wife. "Why are you so distressed?"

"I must return home at once. You'll have to follow me with the children."

Paula took the letter from his hand. She read that serious riots had broken out in Jaffa. Nearly a hundred people, both Jews and Arabs, had been killed.

'Home' to Ben-Gurion meant the Histadruth office in Tel-Aviv. There was only one answer to all this strife and bloodshed—to build quickly, and well; to make the Jewish worker so strong that the Arabs would see he was in Palestine to stay.

As leader of the Histadruth Ben-Gurion had a further worry. After 1924 many thousands of Polish Jews began to enter the country. A large proportion of these were not Socialists at all. They were followers of Vladimir Jabotinsky, who believed the Histadruth had grown too powerful. Sometimes, when Histadruth men went out on strike for more pay, Jabotinsky's supporters would go in and take their jobs.

Yet despite these troubles, Jewish Palestine continued to grow. Pioneers went up to the northernmost tip of Galilee, and to the Jordan Valley, to build their colonies on sand-dunes or in the marshland. A whole stretch of the Vale of Jezreel, just a swamp, was cleansed of the deadly mosquito, and turned into lush farming land, with orange groves, corn-fields and vegetables.

A dozen or more kibbutzim were founded in Jezreel. They produced a tough and independent breed of farmer who was quite capable of looking after himself should there be any attacks from the Arabs.

Just as the Bible prophesied, they were making the desert blossom as the rose. But in addition to this, they became a secret Jewish army. Their bravery and devotion to the cause gave them an important say in the councils of the Histadruth.

Ben-Gurion thought weapon-training was im-mensely important, but he would not put his trust exclusively in the sword. He was a great believer in education and in political work among the British. He was also hopeful that the Histadruth could help the Arab workers too, and so win their friendship.

Year by year, the Histadruth branched out into new fields. It now had many thousands of members, and the workers grew to rely on it for all their needs. Jabotinsky and the private farmers and other employers feared the Histadruth's power. They called it "a state within a state". They said that its leaders were too ambitious. And the man they complained about most was David Ben-Gurion, its General Secretary.

Unable to break the Histadruth's power within Palestine, these people tried other tactics. At the Zionist Congress which took place in Vienna in 1925, there were only 60 Socialist delegates out of 311. Ben-Gurion's opponents thought, therefore, that they could defeat him there. Their plan was to persuade Dr. Weizmann and the other Zionist leaders to cut down on the money which was sent to Palestine for the use of the Histadruth.

Ben-Gurion sat through the Congress sessions, hearing all the complaints against his comrades and himself. Then he went into the attack.

"Let me tell you, gentlemen," he said, speaking quietly at first, then louder and more angrily, "let me tell you that Zionism means nothing if you do not bear in mind that we are building a Jewish nation. What does a nation consist of? It consists of the greatest possible number of *workers*. They are the builders. What the workers set out to do has been achieved. But whatever has been the responsibility of you others has failed!"

Then he reviewed the defeats which the Jews had suffered on the political front: the cutting away of the lands beyond the Jordan and formed by Britain into another country, Transjordan; the law forbidding Jews to buy and settle on that land, even though it was part of Biblical Palestine; and the growth of Arab opposition under their own leader, who was both a politician and a priest, the Mufti of Jerusalem.

"You are supposed to be the leaders of our movement," said Ben-Gurion grimly. "What have you done? You stood meekly by while one obstacle after another was placed before us."

The delegates thought him rude and a little mad.

And they told him so as, after the long meetings, they gathered in groups in the corridors behind the conference-hall. Even some of his own friends thought he had gone too far. One of them, the political secretary of the Histadruth, by name Chaim Arlosoroff, said quite boldly: "If Dr. Weizmann spoke as *he* does we'd have no one at all who could talk with the British."

"This man Ben-Gurion wants to do everything at once," complained another delegate, eyeing the unruly-haired Labour leader as he strode by in his rough, working-man's clothes. "After all, the Balfour Declaration is only eight years old."

Despite Ben-Gurion's outburst, the people who were out to clip the Histadruth's wings got their way —at least for a time. Soon after 1925 the Zionist organisation started to run out of money. And one of the first measures taken to avoid a complete crash was a strict economy drive in all Jewish development of Palestine. This in its turn brought about grave unemployment.

There were other unhappy events that foretold disaster. Drought visited the land. Crops withered and died in 1927 because the long-awaited winter rains held off. Then there was a cruel outbreak of typhoid, a fever which can spread like wildfire. It brought people low in the towns and villages, and there were many deaths.

Somehow almost everything went wrong with Zionism at the same time. Kibbutzim in Galilee and the Vale of Jezreel, founded under terrible conditions of hardship, were disbanded. The citrus

73

C*

harvest failed. Men without jobs came in their hundreds to the Histadruth offices, pressing Ben-Gurion and the others for speedy action. Dr. Weizmann toured Palestine, and saw with his own eyes that hunger and misery stalked the land. That tragic year 1927 seemed to mock every Zionist hope.

From his office window a very despondent Ben-Gurion gazed out on the groups of unemployed in the streets. In other rooms of the same office the staff went about their tasks in similar gloom. Histadruth was on the retreat; political discord was spreading, work on the railways and in house-building was stopped. Impatiently Ben-Gurion rose from his desk and strode along the passageway to where his friend, Berl Katznelsen, was busy writing an editorial for *Davar*, the Histadruth newspaper. Without knocking, he barged into Katznelsen's office and dropped into a chair.

"Berl," he said, "there's a crisis in Palestine. Agreed?"

"Agreed," replied the other, barely looking up from his work.

"Yet we, the workers who are the majority in the *Yishuv**, aren't able to do anything about it."

With tired eyes the writer stared at Ben-Gurion. "Have you a solution, David?" he asked.

"I have. We're helpless because we're divided. Even in the Histadruth we can't forget politics." Then he almost shouted the words: "We must have unity!"

---

*Yishuv was the Hebrew word collectively describing the Jews who resided within Palestine, as those living in the rest of the world were known as *Galuth*, or Diaspora Jewry.

"In that case," said Katznelsen, "we've got to talk to Sprinzak and Arlosoroff. They lead a large group of workers. They can win them over for us."

These two heard Ben-Gurion out patiently. Yes, they too were all for unity, they assured him. But how was this to be achieved?

Arlosoroff put the problem this way: "We dislike your attitude to Dr. Weizmann, the head of our movement. We believe his influence with the British Government is strong just because he is moderate and reasonable. We have to back him up."

Sprinzak nodded his head vigorously. "And we disagree with you when you talk of 'workers fighting employers'. Every Jew who lives and works in Palestine helps our cause, whether he's a worker or an employer. We're not here to fight private farmers and businessmen. We're here to transform this desert land into rich, agricultural country, for every Jew, whatever his class, to be proud of. It will not be done by conflict."

Turning to Katznelsen, Ben-Gurion asked: "Are these reasons enough to keep us divided, Berl?"

Katznelsen had the ability to get right to the heart of the debate. He examined the arguments put so forcibly by the others. Then he showed that these differences, far from being profound, were really only slight.

"Does it matter whether the Jew transforms the land or the land transforms the Jew? We must get it into our heads that both have to be transformed. That is our goal."

The four men fell silent after this remark. It left

little more to be said. Then they shook hands, in the spirit of 'letting bygones be bygones'.

Out of this and further discussion emerged a plan for unity. They took it to a large Histadruth conference in Tel Aviv. The debate went on for more than two weeks, and gave townsmen and kibbutz members, port-workers and Government employees, a chance to air their views. At length agreement was reached. In 1930 the Zionist world heard of the formation of the United Workers' Party. In Hebrew the name was contracted to the word 'Mapai'. A new chapter was opened in the story of the Jewish pioneers of the Holy Land.

The Jews during this tragic period were at their weakest in Palestine, as we have seen. But, at the same time, the Arabs were beginning to assert themselves. In the crowded market-places, in the mosques of Jaffa, and within the walled city of Jerusalem, another world was stirring.

Sir Herbert Samuel, at the time he had been High Commissioner of Palestine a few years earlier, had placed an arch-enemy of the Jews into a position of great power among the Arabs. He was Haj Amin el Husseini, and he was appointed to the religious post of Mufti of Jerusalem. The High Commissioner had not, of course, done this because he opposed Zionism. The contrary was true. But he thought that this would be a gesture that the Arabs would take in friendship. In this way he hoped to win over a man who disliked both the British and the Jews.

Samuel was mistaken. The Mufti grew more arrogant. Hungry for power, he set out to make himself the leader of the Arab world. There was no better way of doing this than by preaching hatred of the Jews.

The man turned out to be a cunning politician. He chose what was obviously the right moment to rouse his people. He inflamed the Arab youth by suggesting that the newcomers intended to take over the holy places of both Christians and Moslems, and rebuild the Temple on the site of the Mosque of Omar, sacred to all followers of Mohammed.

Information reaching the Zionists showed that trouble-makers were planning an attack on the Jewish quarters of Jerusalem. Ben-Zvi was sent to Government House to give the danger signal to Sir John Chancellor, who was then High Commissioner. All other leaders of the Jewish community were at that time away at another Zionist Congress, in Switzerland.

"The situation is well under control," Sir John told Ben-Zvi. "We are perfectly capable of maintaining order."

"Allow the Jews arms to protect themselves," the other implored. "The Arabs won't attack if they know we have means of defence."

"No. That's the job of the British Army and police."

But the worst of Ben-Zvi's fears was realised. Arab gangs fell upon innocent Jews first in Jerusalem, then in Hebron, Haifa and Safed. They used knives and clubs, and slaughtered 140 of them. And the British Army? It came upon the scene too late, after the murderers had retreated.

This pogrom was conducted against religious Jews,

who for the most part lived a way of life untouched by Zionism. The new settlers in the colonies were left unmolested. For the Arabs well knew that these had secret hoards of arms and were more than a match for any street-gang.

The British Government then started an enquiry into the massacres. Grievances were heard from both sides. The Arabs said they were being cheated of their homeland. The Jews insisted that if their warnings had been heeded, there would have been no bloodshed. The sinister Mufti rubbed his hands in full expectation of a coming victory.

He almost got it. The Government, deciding that there was some basis for the Arab fears, ordered a stoppage of immigration for the time being. It forbade the Jews from purchasing more land. This really meant the end of Zionism: no more people, no more land, no more progress. It was as if the Jews were told: "You now have your National Home, as we promised in the Balfour Declaration. There is nothing more to be done."

The Jews closed their ranks. They protested against these orders, and had them toned down. They solved their own money problems with the aid of friends in America. The work went on.

What shocked Ben-Gurion most in all these developments was the fact that a Labour Government in Britain, under the Socialist Prime Minister, Ramsay MacDonald, had tried to put an end to their work. This did not seem to make sense to him. Ben-Gurion, too, was a Socialist, and so were most of the workers in Palestine.

Well, there was a lesson to learn, and Ben-Gurion learned it. It was that henceforth the Jews could rely on no one but themselves. And the Jews would not be safe in Palestine until they were a majority there.

"We shall not surrender," he said. "We shall not seek revenge, and we shall not carry on our work at the expense of our neighbours. We are returning to our land to rebuild our future with our own strength, and in peace."

CHAPTER SEVEN

The Struggle for Jewish Rights

THE man was as good as his word. Jews began to enter Palestine again, and the Yishuv recovered the ground lost by the economic slump and the political troubles which grew out of it. By 1932 the Jewish population reached 150,000, more than one-sixth of the total number of people in Palestine.

Ben-Gurion was the most important Labour leader in Palestine, especially as Mapai, the party formed with Sprinzak's and Arlosoroff's help, was the largest in the country. But he was not yet in command of the whole Zionist movement, whose chief men were chosen every two years by the Zionist Congress. Two million Jewish voters throughout the world sent their delegates to the Congress, and these as a rule were not Socialists.

At the head of the world movement stood Dr. Chaim Weizmann. He was a famous scientist, very highly thought of by the Government in London and the friend of statesmen in all parts of the world. But Ben-Gurion was not quite sure that Weizmann was the right man to lead the movement. In fact he did not think that the movement understood what it should be doing, because most of its members had no intention of coming to Palestine themselves.

This was the difference between Ben-Gurion and his supporters in Palestine, and Weizmann and the Congress: Ben-Gurion believed that their aim should be an independent Jewish state in Palestine, free to bring in as many people as it wished. Weizmann, on the other hand, thought that to talk of a Jewish state was harmful and would arouse the bitter opposition of the Arabs. By going on as they were doing, he said, the Jews would become a majority in the end, and this would give them all the freedom they needed.

Ben-Gurion did not agree. He looked upon Zionism as a race against time. His knowledge of the Arabs told him that they would try and snatch independence from the British before the Jews could gather their strength.

He had another worry. Jabotinsky, who was against the Histadruth, was winning many supporters in the crowded ghettoes of Eastern Europe. Jabotinsky was in favour of a Jewish state, and did not hesitate to say so. But Ben-Gurion thought that his reckless speeches could only end in bloodshed and disaster. Jabotinsky's followers did not bother much about the conquest of the desert. They mostly lived in the cities, and spared little time for the kibbutzim. Suppose Jabotinsky won the next Zionist election? What would happen to the Histadruth and all it had patiently built up since the end of the World War?

For these reasons Ben-Gurion decided in 1932 that

the Jewish workers must gain control of the Zionist Congress. He went to Europe and fought an election campaign that took him to every large city on the Continent, stopping only at the borders of the Soviet Union, where Zionism was forbidden. This campaign was successful. Labour won the largest number of votes, with Weizmann's followers second and Jabotinsky's third. Now Labour would sit on the Executive. Now the Histadruth would have a voice in the topmost councils. It was a victory for Ben-Gurion. He was really in power.

Power came to another man very soon after Ben-Gurion's success. On January 30, 1933, the world learned that Adolf Hitler was the new Chancellor of Germany. If ever Zionism had a justification, it was now, when the cruellest of all Jew-haters closed his grip of iron upon the German people.

As that grip began to tighten around the throat of German Jewry, the Zionists put their differences aside and worked out plans to rescue as many as they could. Chaim Arlosoroff was chosen to go to Germany for this task. Although only thirty-one, he was one of the most brilliant men in the movement, and an especial favourite of Dr. Weizmann's.

He went on his errand of mercy to Berlin, and after a few days returned to Tel-Aviv to report to his colleagues. Then something terrible happened. An unknown gunman shot him dead as he walked with his wife on the beaches of Tel-Aviv. A wave of horror swept the country when the news came out, for the crime seemed as senseless as it was barbaric.

No one has yet been able to discover who committed the murder or why. The police arrested a supporter of Jabotinsky, but he was released through lack of evidence. Nevertheless when Congress met that year in Prague, the workers' delegates could not get it out of their heads that they might be seated in the same meeting-hall as the murderers of their beloved comrade. It was, incidentally, the last Congress which Jabotinsky and his followers attended, for he marched his party out of the hall in protest, alleging that the elections had been conducted unfairly.

Thirty thousand Jews poured into Palestine in that year, fleeing from German persecution. It was the greatest number for ten years. Ben-Gurion chose this moment for what seemed a strange act: he extended the hand of friendship to Jabotinsky. He thought that to keep on quarrelling at a time of such crisis was lunacy.

Secretly, Ben-Gurion travelled to London. He offered a pact to Jabotinsky (his party was known as the 'Revisionists', because they wanted to revise the Balfour Declaration of 1917). The Revisionists could come into the Histadruth provided they ceased to oppose the Zionist Executive.

Jabotinsky agreed. He promised to work with Ben-Gurion for a Jewish state, there would be no more squabbles among the workers, and all effort could be concentrated on the rescue of Jews from Germany. Highly satisfied, Ben-Gurion returned home, the 'peace treaty' in his pocket, to get Histadruth's approval.

But they threw it back in his face! What right, he was asked, had he to 'sell them out' to the murderers of their dead colleague?

Ben-Gurion said: "I believe this agreement will help our cause, and I will not scrap it until every member of the Histadruth has given his view. If the majority are against me, then I will inform Jabotinsky that it is off."

Each one of the thousands of members was handed a voting paper, to say whether he was for the agreement or opposed to it. There was a narrow majority against. Ben-Gurion was embarrassed and angry. "You have sinned against the Histadruth," he cried. But he kept his word. The agreement was torn up.

Forty-two thousand Jews came in 1934 to rebuild their lives broken by the German dictator; sixty-two thousand in 1935. These people changed the entire nature of the Yishuv. They set to work with a fury, starting new industries and villages. Some of these German Jews were able to bring their money with them, and Palestine took on the shape of a busy, confident workshop where the article being created was a new nation.

Ben-Gurion was elected Chairman of the Jewish Agency, as the Zionist Executive had come to be called (Weizmann kept the position of honour as President). In his first speech in this office he said defiantly: "We shall not bow to the will of the new Haman in Germany. We shall bring a million Jews into Palestine."

The sight of so many Jews pouring into the country naturally infuriated one man more than any other— the Mufti of Jerusalem. He was working out a neat little scheme which, if successful, would spell the end of Zionism and the expulsion of the British from

Palestine at one stroke. It was to win the support of the dictator of Italy, Mussolini, in his efforts to become master of Palestine. This suited Mussolini, too, who was having trouble with the League of Nations because of his own plan to seize Abyssinia and become the strong man of the Mediterranean countries.

Ben-Gurion had never spoken with the Mufti, although he had had dealings with other Arabs close to him. And the man who became Jewish Agency Chairman considered it wrong to abandon all hope of coming to terms with the Arabs. He made an effort to meet the Mufti, but failed. Then he wrote a letter to Musa Alami, a highly-respected Arab lawyer in Jerusalem who was, moreover, of the same family as the Mufti.

The letter said: "I should be honoured if you would come to a meeting in my home to discuss how your people and mine can live in peace together in this country, which will one day be an independent state."

Musa Alami came. "What are your terms?" he asked.

"We shall offer the Arabs full equality. We shall develop this country so that it becomes a model for all its neighbours. We shall make it prosperous. You will be as proud of Palestine as we ourselves."

"But what kind of state will Palestine be, Mr. Ben-Gurion?"

"It will be a Jewish state."

There was a long silence. Then the other said: "You ask too much."

Ben-Gurion searched the face of the other as he spoke of the troubles of the Jews, to find some glimmer of understanding there.

"We dare not seek less. Our brothers are in peril in Europe. If we do not save them, no one else will."

"I am afraid I cannot make any promises on behalf of the Arabs. This is too important a question," said Musa Alami, shaking his head.

"Then who else is there to deal with?" Ben-Gurion wanted desperately to succeed.

"We have our office in Geneva. Go there. Talk to the Arabs who do our political work at the League of Nations."

The Jew travelled to Geneva. There were more meetings, but it was of little use. He even suggested making Palestine part of a large grouping of independent Middle Eastern countries.

"Would Palestine be ruled by the Jews?" these Arabs asked him.

"We must be the majority. But you will share in the government of the country."

"The Mufti will have none of it."

Of course the Mufti would have no dealings with the Jews. He was getting stronger every day. So strong, in fact, that in April 1936 he struck. He ordered all Arabs to cease working for the British and the Jews, and he terrorised those who broke the order. Soon shots rang out. At first it was an odd bullet whistling past in the night; then special Arab gunmen were hired from outside Palestine, and murder became a daily commonplace. It was civil war, in which one million Arabs were ranged against four hundred thousand Jews, with the British Army in the midst of them like a man with a water-pistol trying to put out a forest-fire.

The Jews had no desire to attack the Arabs, many of whom had little heart for this bloodshed. The order that went out to the settlements from the Jewish Agency was: "Defend yourselves, but do not attack!"

At last the Government became tired of the Mufti's trouble-making, and decided to put him behind prison-bars. But he was too crafty to allow himself to be captured. He smuggled himself out of the country, to turn up in various capitals of Europe and Asia in later years, still preaching his bitter warfare against the Jews.

It was obvious to the Prime Minister in London, Stanley Baldwin, that the Palestine problem was going to be a hard nut to crack, especially as Hitler was taking even sterner measures against the Jews, and Dr. Weizmann kept demanding the right to bring many more to safety. So Baldwin sent a wise and just public servant, Lord Peel, to Palestine to lead a Commission and bring back proposals for ending the dispute.

Out of this came the famous Peel Report. It weighed Jewish needs against Arab fears, and concluded that the Balfour Declaration had set the Government a hopeless task. The country should be divided into three parts: Britain should keep Jerusalem, Nazareth and an outlet to the sea at Haifa; most of the remainder should be combined with Transjordan to form a large Arab state; and the Jews should be given Galilee and the Vale of Jezreel, together with a small neighbouring area, as an independent state of their own. This country would be about the size of Yorkshire, one-fifth of the area of Western Palestine.

Baldwin announced in the House of Commons that his Government accepted Lord Peel's suggestion, but until it could be carried out not more than twelve thousand Jews might enter Palestine each year.

The Arabs turned the plan down, however, and started their attacks again. The Jews, on the other hand, were split. Many felt that such a tiny state as was offered them could not survive, and that in any case it was quite inadequate to do the urgent job of receiving German Jewry. The religious Jews said a Jewish state without Jerusalem was Zionism without Zion; and the Revisionists cried bitterly that the whole idea was a mockery.

What did the leaders say? Weizmann, that great Jewish patriot, must have searched deep within himself before he spoke. Then he said: "I believe we should try and make the plan work." The result was a torrent of protest. It seemed that the more people studied the scheme, the more they hated it. Now all the Histadruth leaders were ranged against it, too. All, that is, except one man. He had not yet given his verdict.

The Chairman of the Jewish Agency was waiting for the Zionist Congress, due to meet for the twentieth time in August 1937. Then Ben-Gurion, in one of his greatest speeches, put himself by the side of Weizmann.

"After two thousand years of slavery, of exile, of persecution, the Government of a mighty empire, holding the destiny of Palestine, proposes that we have our own state in our own land. . . . One-fifth of Palestine, it is true, but nevertheless containing nearly the entire seaboard. This means that the Jewish people, for the first time in its history, has an opportunity to become a people of the sea. Just as we took root in the soil despite centuries of landlessness, so shall we master the sea even though we have never been a seafaring people."

He went on to tell the objectors: "Just four centuries ago Britain, the great nation whose ships today sail all the oceans, was confined within the borders of a small island."

Ben-Gurion silenced the opposition with these words. What many Zionists had been afraid to say— that they should have a Jewish state—Britain had said for them, once and for ever. It might not happen at once. It could take years. But freedom in their own state they would one day have.

Alas! there would be many obstacles to overcome before that historic day would dawn. Events immediately began to take place which caused Britain to forget her promise.

The League of Nations, formed after the war of 1914-1918 to safeguard the peace of the world, was crumbling away. First Italy, then Germany defied it. The statesmen of Europe looked anxiously at the gathering clouds of war, and gave in to almost every demand of the dictators in a vain effort to avoid a storm.

With so many other problems on her hands, Britain kept postponing a decision in Palestine. Ben-Gurion's London office was in Bloomsbury, almost next door to the British Museum. He would sit there hour after hour, as reports came in of the hell in which German Jews were suffering.

"We must get them away. We *must!*" he cried. Then he would go to Whitehall, to speak to the Colonial Secretary, who was in charge of Palestine affairs.

"If you will grant us permission, we can transport thousands of our people to safety in Palestine. Otherwise it may be too late," he would tell the Minister.

"We dare not. With the temper of the Arab people as it is at present, we can only allow a few hundred in each year."

"Does the mighty British Empire retreat because of the anger of a handful of rebels?"

"The British Empire has work to do in many places. Palestine is only a small part of our responsibilities. Too many soldiers are being kept there already."

This kind of fruitless discussion was repeated so often that the Jews in the end stopped asking for permission. They started to smuggle their people out of Europe and into Palestine by means of a secret organisation. In charge of it were heroic young men and women guides who would stop at nothing to attain their objective. Mysterious ships moved across the Mediterranean by night, and their passengers melted away into tiny craft that landed them on the open beaches.

Hitler swallowed Austria, then turned his attentions to Czechoslovakia. More Jews homeless; more in concentration camps; more tragedy everywhere. The long night of suffering had begun. The Government called a conference at St. James's Palace in London in one more, last effort to avoid disaster in Palestine. But the Arabs would not talk with the Jews. Then Lord Halifax, who was the Foreign Secretary, made this announcement:

"We have decided to turn Palestine into an independent state some time in the next ten years. Jews will be allowed to go there only during the next five years, and not more than seventy-five thousand altogether."

This meant in fact an Arab state, with the Jews in the minority—at the mercy of others. It would finish the Jewish National Home.

Ben-Gurion, on behalf of his colleagues, answered the Foreign Secretary. He spoke slowly, his voice shaking with anger. "You will not do it, except with your bayonets." With this challenge the conference broke up.

Within a few short months the war everyone dreaded burst with shattering force upon Europe. But in Palestine, Britain acted as if nothing had happened. She began to put the new regulations into effect. The Jews could not buy land in Palestine, nor bring their people there. The Government put all this into an official document, known as the Palestine White Paper, just as Hitler invaded the Low Countries, conquered Paris and made himself master of practically all Western Europe.

By the summer of 1940 the British people alone stood in the path of Hitler's plans for world-conquest. Under the inspiration of Winston Churchill, and despite the great hardships caused them, they kept the war going against the tyrant. Jews everywhere saw that without Britain's victory they themselves had no chance of survival. They admired Britain for her heroic struggle, and whenever possible they fought with her, shoulder to shoulder against the common enemy. And those who were not in a position to fight, because they were slaves in Europe, prayed for the success of her arms.

Yet they had also to oppose Britain's policy in Palestine. For Britain barred the way to safety for masses of Jews crying for shelter. It was a strange and tragic situation. Ben-Gurion summed it up in a famous sentence which served as a rallying-call to the Zionist movement during the years of strife. "We shall fight the war," he said, "as if there were no White Paper, and the White Paper as if there were no war."

CHAPTER EIGHT

Tragic Happenings

EARLY in the summer of 1940, Dr. Chaim Weizmann, the President of the Zionist Organisation, and David Ben-Gurion, Chairman of the Jewish Agency for Palestine, boarded a taxi outside their London headquarters.

"To the Colonial Office," Weizmann ordered the driver.

In the space of a few minutes they were at the department in charge of Palestine affairs, and quickly they were ushered by a clerk into the office of the Minister. His name was Lord Lloyd. The two visitors greeted him with every politeness, but without warmth. They knew that Lord Lloyd considered Zionism to be wrong and believed that it was a mistake on the part of the Government to encourage it. But he welcomed them cordially enough.

"Please be seated, gentlemen," he said.

Dr. Weizmann came to the point. "We have come to ask for the creation of a Jewish army," he said. "Our people regard this struggle against Germany as their struggle. They want to join in the war. They are queueing in their hundreds at our recruiting offices in Palestine. How do you propose to use them?"

"We are dealing with this matter," answered the Minister. "The idea we have in mind is to enrol equal numbers of Jews and Arabs in Palestine regiments."

"But surely you must realise that the Arabs are unwilling to join up," Weizmann protested. "They are swallowing Hitler's propaganda utterly. They do not want Britain to win the war!"

"I regret, Dr. Weizmann, that the reports from our men on the spot do not bear this out," Lloyd said, with an icy smile.

Ben-Gurion then spoke up. "We have half a million people there," he said. "If they were British by blood and language they could not be more reliable. If there is trouble between us the fault lies with your officials."

The interview came to an end, with nothing promised. As they left the building, Ben-Gurion said to his colleague: "We must warn Britain that if she expects our support in the war, and the help of the Jews of Palestine—not to mention America—she must tear up the White Paper."

"We'll get nothing from that man," observed Weizmann sadly. "He hates us."

"No, he disagrees with us, and that's something different. There are others who hate us much more, and that's why we can't put our views before Winston Churchill."

The war was going badly for Britain. First Norway, then the Low Countries, then France herself had been crushed by Hitler's war machine. Italy joined in against Britain, and so the war was spread to the Mediterranean. In July, Lord Lloyd asked Ben-Gurion to come and see him again, and the latter thought that this was his chance.

"Now that Italy has declared war the Suez Canal is in danger," he said. "Why not use Palestine to the utmost?"

"What are your suggestions, Mr. Ben-Gurion?"

"In addition to the large number of soldiers we could give you, we have our factories. We could manufacture arms and medicines. We have Jewish Agency men in neutral countries such as Turkey, and they could bring you information about the enemy."

It was no use. "All this would upset the Arabs too much, and give us a great deal of trouble," Lloyd replied.

The months dragged by, and still the demand for a Jewish army met with a strong refusal. Ben-Gurion continued to see the Minister, and even grew to like him. They discussed every aspect of the war, not only the part affecting Palestine. Sometimes Lord Lloyd appeared distressed, and on such occasions Ben-Gurion encouraged him. "For Britain to be facing the threat of destruction is strange and new," he once said. "But we've been facing it for two thousand years, yet we survived."

Zionism had friends, not only opponents, among the British. One of these was a brave soldier named Orde Wingate, who had been in trouble while he was an Army officer in Palestine for helping the Jewish self-defence units. Wingate came to Ben-Gurion with the request that he be sent to Palestine to form a

Jewish army. The Jewish Agency Chairman put this to Lloyd.

"I like Wingate," said Lloyd. "But if we give him a job among your people in Palestine the Arabs would be up in arms."

It was always the same reply—the Arabs, the Arabs. "We're only concerned with winning the war," Ben-Gurion urged. "We need victory as much, if not more than you."

"There's one thing you can do, Mr. Ben-Gurion, that will have greater effect than all your pressure upon the Government."

"I'm ready. What is it?"

"Go to America and talk to your people there about our cause. The United States is not as friendly as we would wish."

"I'll go at once."

Living in London at this most critical period of the war for Britain, with nightly bombing-raids upon London, food shortages and the entire nation alerted in the daily expectation of a German invasion from the Continent, taught Ben-Gurion a new respect for the British people.

Before leaving for New York he sent a note to Dr. Weizmann and all his other Jewish Agency colleagues as follows: "We should take to heart what the British have been teaching the world in recent months. This is, never to accept defeat."

America was not yet in the war, and most Americans were of course hoping that their country never would be. This applied to the Jews too. Ben-Gurion explained to the Zionist leaders across the

Atlantic that they could bring a Jewish army nearer if Jews joined up in larger numbers for Britain. And a Jewish army, he emphasised, brought the hope of a Jewish state much nearer.

In the meantime, what had been happening in Palestine during Ben-Gurion's absence? Jews were enlisting in the British forces, rather than wait for their own special army. Moshe Shertok was in charge of the recruitment. At the same time, the Government carried out the White Paper policy to the letter, just as it had threatened to do. This made every kind of Zionist work difficult, and the Jewish population was involved in constant conflict with their British masters.

"We shall fight the war as if there were no White Paper," Ben-Gurion had said, "and the White Paper as if there were no war." This indeed was happening. For while Shertok urged his people to join the British Army, and Ben-Gurion and Weizmann were urging the Government to use the Jews to the utmost, others were planning ways of stiffening the Yishuv's resistance towards the hated laws of the Colonial Office. They formed the old self-defence guards into a compact force, which they named Haganah.

Ben-Gurion had a will of iron, and now, under the stress of war, it was beginning to show itself more than ever before. He thought nothing mattered so much as the Jewish army, which must be brought into being. Suddenly, at the end of 1941, he saw his chance. The Japanese, by their sudden treacherous attack on the American naval base of Pearl Harbour, brought the United States, willy-nilly, into the struggle.

D

What did this mean to the Zionist leader? First, the certainty that, sooner or later, Germany would be defeated. Secondly, that the very large American Jewish community would strengthen his hand in the political battle with Britain over the White Paper. And, third, that Britain would not be able to hold out against the idea of a Jewish army, because he would go back to America and get the Jews over there to raise their voice for it in a way that was not possible before.

This he did. Five million Jews lived in America, and they could make themselves felt. Zionism took on a new lease of life, and the call went out that, as soon as the war was over, Palestine should be turned into a Jewish state. In the end, something of the mood of American Jewry reached the ears of Winston Churchill. He ordered his War Minister to form Jewish volunteers into a separate fighting group, under their own officers.

It had taken five long years to win this right, but it proved an important victory just the same. The Jewish Brigade, as it was called, took part in the conquest of Italy in 1944, and moved into Germany when the war reached its climax and the Nazis were brought to their knees.

The war in Europe ended on May 7, 1945. What a cruel reckoning there was for Jewry! After the victory marches and the welcome home of the conquering heroes, it was found that some five million Jews had lost their lives. Those who had lived through the hell of it all were nearly-broken men and women or pitiful orphans. Ben-Gurion himself toured the concentration camps, to give hope to these innocent victims.

"During these six years of war," he told them, "we never forgot you for a single day. We have been working to build up our land so that you may come there, to live as decent human beings again, among your own people, where you will not fear again!"

He spoke too soon. A new Government of Socialists was formed in Britain. The Foreign Secretary was Ernest Bevin, and when the Jewish leaders came to him with the request that they now be allowed to form their own state and bring their people into it, they found him harder than any British statesman they had ever dealt with before.

Bevin had no intention of creating a Jewish state. As far as he was concerned, the White Paper policy was still in force. He and Ben-Gurion fought the matter out face-to-face, with neither giving way on a single point. But Bevin had the power. He sent large numbers of British troops into Palestine to keep the Jews in check. He despatched the Navy to patrol the coast-line of Palestine and capture the ships carrying refugees.

There were tragic scenes on the high seas between desperate Jews and these servants of Bevin. The British Foreign Secretary refused to admit that the Jews had any rights in Palestine at all, and he blamed America for encouraging them and so causing so much trouble for Britain. And, more serious still, armed Jewish groups in Palestine were becoming impatient with their leaders. They began to take matters into their own hands, so that before long a sort of undeclared war between the Yishuv and the British broke out.

The Holy Land knew no peace. Bombs shattered famous buildings in Jerusalem and the country was turned into an armed camp. The British Government accused the Jewish leaders of rebellion. This was not true. The only people who were in open revolt against Britain belonged to two groups, which were a law unto themselves. The more important of the two was called Irgun Zvai Leumi (Irgun, for short); it was led by a newcomer to Palestine, Menachem Beigin. The other was smaller in size, but even more fierce in its hatred of Britain, and was called, after its founder, the Stern Group. These people hardly ever bothered to inform the Jewish Agency of their plans. They disliked the way Ben-Gurion and his colleagues handled Zionist affairs, and they were much quicker on the trigger than were the Haganah men, who took their instructions only from the Agency.

But to Ernest Bevin all the Jews were tarred with the same brush. He would not see any difference between Haganah and the Irgun. And when his soldiers failed to restore order in Palestine, he suddenly swooped upon all the Agency leaders he could find and put them behind barbed wire.

Among those to be taken away was Moshe Shertok, the man who had done so much to enrol Jews in the British Army when Britain was fighting alone. So great was Bevin's fury! But there was one important leader—the most important—that he could not get his hands on. This was Ben-Gurion. The Jewish Agency Chairman was in London at the time.

There he got wind of what was about to take place. And, quietly, he slipped across the Channel, to a secret hiding-place in Paris.

What was the cause of Bevin's cruel obstinacy? He was, after all, a Socialist like so many of the pioneers in Palestine. But he did not think as a Socialist when dealing with the Palestine problem. He thought instead of the oil of the Middle East, and the Suez Canal through which this precious fuel was brought to Europe. And when he weighed the Jews against these vital British interests, he came to the conclusion that, to save the latter, it was better to abandon the Jews.

Whatever the causes, it was a grim situation. In Paris, Ben-Gurion directed the affairs of the Zionist movement from a small building not far from the Arc de Triomphe. He and his followers worked night and day, keeping in touch with Haganah, making secret journeys across Europe, sending messages in code.

Sometimes, exhausted from their labours, his followers came back to Ben-Gurion in fits of depression.

"How will it all end, David?" they asked him. "Britain is a mighty Power, and the Arabs, too, are getting stronger. We have only six hundred thousand people in Palestine."

"It will end in the creation of a Jewish state, and in four or five years at that." Ben-Gurion said this in 1946. The prophecy was to be proved correct sooner even than he dreamed possible.

After a few months Bevin tried another tack. He

freed the Zionist prisoners in Palestine. He invited them to come to London for talks. He brought Arab spokesmen to London, too. It seemed like history repeating itself. Of course, the Arabs would not meet the Jews. The discussions were fruitless. Ben-Gurion and Bevin had a private meeting. Still it was no use. They could not speak together for more than a few minutes. Bevin would not budge.

"We cannot give in to your demands," he told Ben-Gurion, "because they would lead to the end of our friendship with the Arab people."

"You're losing that anyway, Mr. Bevin. We Jews wish to be your friends. We've always been allied together. But there's no hope in your present policy."

Of course there wasn't. In the end, Bevin had to do what many statesmen, among them Winston Churchill, had begged him to do months before. He had to take the problem to the United Nations.

At the British Foreign Secretary's request, a special meeting took place at the New York headquarters in the spring of 1947. Such a meeting could be held only if there was a matter to discuss affecting world peace, so it will be seen how serious the problem of Palestine had become.

Important statesmen of many nationalities suddenly had to read up the history of the case. Up till then, the Middle East and its peoples had been mostly left to Britain to deal with, and, to a lesser extent, France and America. This was now changed. Once the United Nations had the subject in hand, Britain ceased to be the judge of the Arab-Jewish quarrel. She would have to take orders about what to do, not give them.

Machine-guns crackled in Jerusalem. Ships carrying Jewish refugees were captured by sailors of the Royal Navy. Soldiers raided the settlements, searching for arms. Palestine was on the brink of disaster. These were the happenings in the minds of the statesmen as they talked on. Ben-Gurion came to the council-chamber, to state his case before the various committees. Moshe Shertok accompanied him, and an important American Zionist and rabbi named Abba Hillel Silver. Of course, the Arab nations had their spokesmen, too. As the debate proceeded, the excitement rose to fever-pitch.

The United Nations chose eleven men, each from a different country, to examine the problem afresh on the spot. Ben-Gurion returned to Jerusalem, to be on call for questioning. It became clear to him that a decision of immense importance was about to be made.

Finally, on November 29, 1947, the United Nations, having thoroughly gone through the report of the eleven investigators, came to this decision: "Britain must leave Palestine by August 1, 1948. Two states, one Arab, one Jewish, must be created in the course of the following two months."

The British Government said: "We accept the decision. We shall end our Mandate on May 15."

Ben-Gurion was taking a short rest at an hotel on the shores of the Dead Sea when he heard the news on the radio. He left at once for the Jewish Agency headquarters in Jerusalem. There he was greeted by thousands of wildly cheering people. "We have won a great victory," he told them. "This is an historic hour for our people."

The Arabs were furious at the result. "If the Jews attempt to carry out this plan," they threatened, "we shall rise and drive them into the sea."

Thus, in the midst of the triumph, new dangers beset the Yishuv. That old enemy of the Jews, the former Mufti of Jerusalem, tried to carry out the threat almost at once. From his exile he sent armed bands into Palestine. They were met by mortar-fire from Haganah. Every able-bodied Jew had his orders.

David Ben-Gurion was the leader of a people that numbered little more than six hundred thousand men, women and children. Before long they would be on their own in Palestine, with the right to form a state if they dared, but without anybody's help except the goodwill of the United Nations. The British Army was soon to move out, leaving the Jews to fend for themselves. On all sides, and right in the midst of them, the Arabs waited.

The day of decision drew closer. Even some of Ben-Gurion's closest friends wondered whether it would be right for the Jews to take up the challenge, defy the hatred of the Arabs and found their state on May 15. Messages were received from abroad that the United States Government, which had at first strongly favoured the idea of dividing Palestine between the Jews and Arabs, had now changed its mind.

Somehow, these doubts seemed of little moment to the man who, in Tel-Aviv, was already setting up an Army Command, nominating his generals and making his plans to occupy, step-by-step, the land awarded the Jews as the British soldiers left. The situation was not too hopeful. Jerusalem was surrounded by armed Arabs who would not allow food-lorries to reach its inhabitants. They even had the water supply of the Holy City at their mercy.

At the end of March, some six weeks before the British were due to hand over the reins of government, Ben-Gurion showed to the world a new type of Jew: a fighter who would gladly risk his life for the land which was the centre of all his prayers.

Ben-Gurion ordered his men to shoot their way through to Jerusalem. This meant advancing along a perilous road for forty-five miles of hilly territory under the guns of the enemy, who occupied the heights. After a fierce and costly battle, the Jews were victorious. Triumphantly the truck-loads of food, ammunition and medical supplies rumbled their way up to the western outskirts of the city, and Jerusalem was saved.

Not every battle went as well as this one. There were tragic losses in the scattered settlements down south, and on the road leading to the Hebrew University high over Jerusalem on Mount Scopus. The Arabs showed no mercy when on top, but when faced with determined opposition they were seen to lose heart.

What would Ben-Gurion do on May 15? There was, in his mind, only one course to take. The work begun when, forty-two years earlier, he landed at Jaffa harbour as a humble pioneer, must now be completed.

D*

CHAPTER NINE

Ben-Gurion Leads his People to Victory

IN a sand-bagged villa on the outskirts of Tel-Aviv, the short, grey-haired man who now had the destiny of a people in his charge sat poring over a map. He was sixty-two years of age, though as sturdy as a youth. He had kept himself fit through the years of struggle by living simply, caring not a jot for earthly luxuries. Ben-Gurion had never been a smoker, and his favourite drink was a glass of tea with lemon. Now this vigour was to serve him in good stead.

With him studying the map were half a dozen other, mostly younger, men. Just as he was not yet a Prime Minister, they were not yet generals. Some of them were kibbutz-members, one was an engineer, another an archaeologist. But whatever their occupations, their lives had up till then had a secret side: soldiering. Now that secret side was to come out into the open.

The United Nations had ordered that the Jewish state to be brought into being on May 15 would consist of the coastal plain of Palestine roughly from a point 15 miles south of Tel-Aviv to a point just north of Haifa. To this was to be joined the eastern half of Galilee and almost all the southern area of the country, a desert region known as the Negev. Western Galilee and Samaria, in addition to the Gaza area, were awarded to the Arabs to form their state. Jerusalem and its near surroundings, together with Bethlehem, was to belong to neither of them, but to be kept in trust by the United Nations under a special Governor.

All this was marked out on the map in front of Ben-Gurion. The Arabs had of course stated that they would not accept the plan, for they wanted the whole country. Only the Jews had agreed, but Ben-Gurion knew that like so many others, it would never be anything else but a plan unless they were ready to hold on to their part of the country by force when the time came for dividing Palestine.

"We must not give up a single point," he declared. "Every kibbutz must be held, every road kept open."

His companions admired and loved their leader. They were prepared to follow him to the death. But they had studied the military situation very closely, and they were not too sure of the strength of those opposing them.

"We have no guns," they reminded him.

"But they're on the way," he replied. "Our agents have been buying guns, as well as aircraft, in France and Czechoslovakia."

"If they come in time—so much the better," one of the group said. "But we must base our plans on the weapons we already possess. All we have are rifles and sten-guns, a few hundred machine-guns, mortars and

grenades—not to mention our old-fashioned 'kites'."
There was laughter at this remark, for those aeroplanes
really were old-fashioned. The British had allowed
the Jews to have them for a flying-club, which was
about all they were good for.

Ben-Gurion snapped out a few orders which soon
silenced the laughter. "Make sure that every able-
bodied man can use a rifle. And enlist as many women
as possible. Take over all cars and lorries. Wherever
the British leave a building or an army camp, seize it!"

"Sir, some of our villages are so spread out that it
will be difficult to hold them."

"We *must* hold them. There's no choice. If we
retreat, we shall soon find ourselves in the sea."

It was now the beginning of May. The khaki uniform of the British soldier, a familiar sight throughout
Palestine for some thirty years, was now to be seen
only in the neighbourhood of Haifa, where the
troops were busy embarking for home. There was no
police-force now, no delivery of mail, no law-courts.
Nothing that was the duty of a Government to perform was being done.

The Jews, however, had no intention of being caught
napping. As the chaos grew with the end of British
rule, they put some of their own long-laid schemes for
running affairs into operation. Thirty-seven leading
Palestinian members of the Zionist movement, from
all parties, formed a 'shadow' Parliament. Twelve of
these had been quietly setting up various offices to
take charge of home and foreign affairs, education,
finance, transport and other needs. They became the
'shadow' Jewish Government.

Early on Friday morning, May 14, the British High Commissioner, Sir Alan Cunningham, left his official residence in Jerusalem and flew in his private plane to Haifa. The Union Jack was hauled down. That same afternoon a messenger came to Ben-Gurion's villa. He handed a note to the young Jew guarding the door.

This note was taken to the man seated with his advisers in an upstairs room. When he read it, Ben-Gurion announced to the others. "All is ready. Let's go."

Their destination was only a few minutes away by car. It was the Tel-Aviv Museum, and waiting there were about two hundred people—those who formed the State Council, high officials of the Jewish Agency, important foreign visitors, and correspondents of the world's newspapers.

Ben-Gurion waited till exactly four o'clock. Then, in his firm, clear voice, he read the Proclamation of Independence.

"We hereby declare that, as from the termination of the Mandate, at midnight this night, the National Administration shall constitute the Provisional Government of the Jewish State, which shall be known as Israel."

The voice went on, evenly, unfalteringly, as it uttered the historic words: "We appeal to the United Nations to assist the Jewish people in the building of their state. . . . We appeal to the Arab inhabitants to preserve the ways of peace. . . . To the Jews all over the world our call goes out to rally to our side. . . . With trust in Almighty God, we set our hand to this Declaration, at this session of the Provisional State Council, on the soil of the Homeland, in the city of

Tel-Aviv, on this Sabbath Eve, Iyar 5, 5708, May 14, 1948."

First Ben-Gurion, then the thirty-six other members of the 'Parliament' signed the Proclamation. Out rushed the newspaper correspondents, to telephone or cable the news to their editors.

Many of those left in the Museum wept, in happiness and in pride. They felt they were witnessing history being made. For the words spoken by the Jewish leader meant that the die was cast. After two thousand years of wandering, of persecution, of being among alien peoples, Israel was a nation again.

But would she remain a nation? Millions of people throughout the world thought that she would not. It depended, they said, on what the Arab states would do—not the armed bands of the Mufti, skulking on the hillsides, but the Governments which shared their frontiers with Israel, and had armies, tanks, bombing-planes, warships.

At dawn the next day Egyptian aircraft swooped across the Sinai desert, their shadows looking like giant birds of prey on the sand. This confirmed the worst fears in the minds of the doubters. For they were bombers, come to drop their deadly loads upon the city of Tel-Aviv. The war was on in earnest.

The Arab rulers had indeed decided to carry out their threat to drive the Jews into the sea. Later that day the Egyptian Army moved. It formed into two great prongs, advancing on Tel-Aviv and Beersheba. At the same time a strong force of Transjordanians, the proud Arab Legion which had been raised from desert tribesmen and trained by British officers, crossed the River Jordan and sped towards Jerusalem. Travelling swiftly in their armoured cars, they almost encircled the city.

Out of Syria poured hosts of soldiers bent upon the easy conquest of Galilee. On their southern flank were the Iraqis, who planned to overrun the Jewish settlements in the Vale of Jezreel and then drive forward to the coast near Haifa. On Palestine's northern border troops of the Lebanon began to mass.

The people who now called themselves Israelis understood that in order to make their Proclamation live, some of them would have to die.

Behind the Arab soldiers were forty million people to urge them on. It seemed a hopeless situation. Yet from the first moment the over-confident invaders blundered. The King of Egypt ordered his warships to patrol the coast, but they were slow in leaving the port of Alexandria and steaming up the Mediterranean. This enabled a large number of cargo vessels with supplies of arms and food for the Israelis to slip into Haifa Bay at night. As a result, Ben-Gurion, who was not only the Prime Minister of the young state but also the Commander-in-Chief of the Army, was able to keep his rifles firing for a few days, to keep his trucks on the roads, and to save his people from starvation.

The Arabs made all kinds of bragging statements of the damage they were inflicting upon the Israelis, but in fact the opposite was true. The land forces of the Egyptian King Farouk were halted at the first sign of serious opposition, and were then led into a trap in the Negev. They did not succeed in escaping from this until the end of the war, when they were let out during a ceasefire. Haifa was taken over by the Israelis even before the last British soldier had left, and from there they swept northward, actually capturing a few villages in the Lebanon.

When their state was barely three days old, the amazed and delighted citizens of Tel-Aviv watched from their roof-tops as fighter planes with blue and white markings attacked the Egyptian bombers. The dog-fights did not last long, for the Egyptians turned tail, never to return.

Ben-Gurion had told his people over the radio: "We shall have weapons and aircraft. They are on the way." He had kept his word. It gave them renewed trust in their Prime Minister.

Victory on the battlefield was important. But so was victory in the political struggle. Ben-Gurion waited anxiously to see what the Powers across the seas would do about his Proclamation of Independence. On May 15 and May 17, two countries, the world's greatest Powers, gave Israel recognition. They were America and the Soviet Union, and by so doing they showed that they accepted the Proclamation in international law.

With his hand thus strengthened, Ben-Gurion toured the battlefronts to be with his beloved soldiers. From time to time he boarded a tiny aeroplane to encourage the citizens of Jerusalem. These people were cut off from the rest of the Jewish community except for a rough and narrow road which proved costly in lives and trucks every time the Jews attempted to pass along it.

The Arabs fell back, and promptly quarrelled among themselves about who was to blame for the failure of their plans. This division in their counsels, bad for the Arab soldiers, proved even more disastrous for the civilians. These unhappy victims of their rulers' policy fled in panic wherever the Jews advanced and seized control. They cleared out of Jaffa and Acre. The wealthier ones, who had settled among the Jews in the newer parts of Jerusalem, crossed into the Old City and then got as far away from the firing-line as their motor-cars could carry them. The poor of Ramleh and Lydda took to the hills. The Jews did not expect the Arabs to depart so hurriedly. But were relieved nevertheless to see them go.

Ben-Gurion was in two minds at first about what he should do in Jerusalem. For some time there was a ding-dong battle between his troops and the Arab Legion, with neither side gaining the advantage for long. Here a peculiar situation had arisen. The city was supposed to be under the charge of the United Nations, and yet the United Nations had failed to protect it. But a hundred thousand Jews lived there. Could they be left to the mercy of the Arab Legion? Of course not!

A small group of four hundred Jews were fighting a desperate rearguard battle to hold the ancient Jewish quarter of the Old City. The rest was in the hands of the Arabs. Ben-Gurion decided on a frontal attack on the Old City, to drive the Legion out of its well-protected positions and unify Jerusalem in one stroke. This was a very dangerous operation, made even more difficult because members of the Irgun and the Stern Group were fighting there too, and, as we have seen, they did not regard Ben-Gurion as their commander.

The Haganah chief was therefore given the task of capturing the Old City without knowing really who was available to do the job. It was eventually taken on by the splendid troops from the kibbutzim, known as the Palmach. These latter, fighting like tigers, forced a way through but could not hold their positions. They were barred by a tremendous volley of machine-gun and artillery fire, and the handful of Jews within the walls, reduced to near-starvation, short of water and low in spirit, were forced to surrender.

What a sad day this was for Israel, and for all Jewry! Those ancient stones of the Old City, where Jews had prayed in an unbroken stream of time for countless centuries, were torn from them. They had defied a ring of steel, as it blazed forth its fire, with a few rifles and home-made grenades. Rabbis had fought bravely side by side with young boys and girls, in tiny alleyways and behind mounds of rubble, sharing every hardship. And it had been of no avail.

The Prime Minister reported on these events to the State Council. Sorrowfully he told the Council of the suffering of Jerusalem. "There have been few encounters in our history where the ordeal was so frightful and the courage so high." But almost in the same breath he showed that, whatever the cost, they would not give up the rest of the city.

"It stands, cut off from all help from us, under the shadow of hunger and thirst, bombarded day and night by those who mock the very meaning of the word

Jerusalem, which is called holy by the Moslems and Christians alike. The Jews there resist because they know that we are with them in our thoughts. The flower of our youth will give their lives for Jerusalem."

He sent his bombers to Amman, the capital of Transjordan, from which the Arab Legion had come. With renewed vigour his troops drove the Syrians and Lebanese right out of Israel. The Arabs began to tremble. They lost heart. They had not reckoned with Jews so skilled in war.

The man in command spared no one, just as he gave the whole of himself to the struggle. He summoned his field commanders to headquarters, to find out where the weakness that had led to the fall of the Old City lay.

"We are commanders only in name," they complained. "Some of our front-line soldiers, even the best of them, will not obey our orders."

Ben-Gurion's face clouded over in anger when he heard this. He was ashamed to have to admit they were right. The soldiers of the Irgun and the Stern Group followed their own leaders only. True, they fought bravely, but sometimes their bravery was wasted because they refused to join with Haganah. Even the Palmach often acted without consulting the Haganah Command.

"Only a united army, loyal to one Government, obeying a single High Command, can resist a foreign invader," said Ben-Gurion with heat. "This is a problem we shall have to settle without delay." The question was, how? The answer was soon to be made known to every citizen of the newly born state.

In the meantime, how were the nations of the world, who had voted for the creation of Israel, looking upon the storm that had blown up in Palestine? The situation filled them with dismay. They sent a representative to Palestine to persuade the two sides to agree to a truce. This was Count Folke Bernadotte. He was a member of the Swedish Royal Family and, through his work in the Red Cross, had already won a reputation for his fearlessness and devotion to peace.

Bernadotte went out to Palestine determined to bring the warring peoples together. Unfortunately, he was not very well-informed on the troubled situation in the Holy Land, and he never succeeded in winning the confidence of either side. Bernadotte's orders were to obtain a cease-fire with the least possible delay. Using a motor-car painted white all over, with the letters U.N. on it, he travelled across the firing-line at grave personal risk. Sometimes he would use his white aeroplane, flying from Damascus to Cairo, then to Tel-Aviv, then to Amman. He never rested and eventually, on June 11, 1948, he succeeded in getting a truce. The opposing armies undertook to silence their weapons for four weeks, and they signed an agreement not to add to their strength by importing war material from overseas. Conditions of this nature are extremely difficult to keep, for the art of war is to outwit your enemy and drive hard against him with all speed, using every possible advantage. Some people in Israel thought Ben-Gurion was mistaken in accepting these conditions just at this moment. A great quantity of armaments was on its way to relieve the Jews' dire shortage of weapons, and thousands of immigrants had begun to pour into the country now that the British White Paper had been torn up. Those newcomers could be valuable recruits for the fighting forces.

But the Prime Minister knew that he dared not defy the United Nations, even though it had let him down by not protecting Israel when the Arabs had revealed their intentions. This brought him to an open clash with the Irgun, who chose this truce as their chance to challenge his authority as head of the state.

The Irgun Zvai Leumi not only fought the war in its own way. It brought its own weapons into the country in order to keep its troops supplied. And, just before the truce was signed, its leaders had arranged for a heavy shipment of arms to reach them from across the seas. This cargo was aboard a ship called the *Altalena,* and three days after the cease-fire she was steaming steadily towards the coast of Israel.

Imagine, therefore, the cruel dilemma facing Prime Minister Ben-Gurion. He needed the arms desperately, and there were plenty aboard the *Altalena* to distribute over several fronts, not simply among the Irgun men. In fact, Menahem Beigin, the latter's leader, was agreeable to a share-out. But if he allowed the ship to dock Ben-Gurion would be breaking his word to Bernadotte. This could easily start up the war again with himself in the wrong, and also show that his authority was not strong enough to impose upon the Irgun. If he let Beigin get away with it this time, who could know when this man would defy him again?

He ordered the ship to keep away. Beigin, who was

in touch with the captain by radio from Tel-Aviv, signalled a message to approach. Ben-Gurion warned Beigin: "We shall regard anyone who breaks the law of the state as a traitor. We shall punish him as an enemy within the ranks."

This could mean the firing-squad. But it did not stop Beigin. He made his way down to the beach, was rowed out to the *Altalena,* and pressed on.

The entire nation waited in suspense for the outcome. This included the soldiers both of Haganah and Irgun, strung along the coast for several miles and bearing opposing instructions. Then the worst happened.

Ben-Gurion ordered his shore-batteries to open fire on the *Altalena.* After a couple of salvoes the ship burst into flames. A large group of Irgun people sprang from her decks on to a tank-landing craft, and were rounded up on the beach a few miles north of Tel-Aviv. Others escaped to specially arranged hiding-places. Fighting between the rival groups on the coast broke out. Twelve men were left dead on the *Altalena.*

It had been Jew against Jew. One of the dead was a man whose name had a familiar ring. He was Abraham Stavsky and, exactly fifteen years earlier, he had been on trial for his life for the murder of Chaim Arlosoroff. It was like a chapter out of some horror-drama, with the events repeating themselves to haunt the memory of the actors.

The nation was deeply divided over Ben-Gurion's stern action. It heard both sides of the story, because Beigin, having escaped from a frightful death on the *Altalena* as thousands of rounds of ammunition exploded, reached a hide-out in Tel-Aviv where he had his secret radio-station. "We've lost five thousand rifles," he broadcast, "nine tanks, hundreds of other weapons. I tried to come to an agreement with the Government. These arms might have meant the difference between victory and defeat for Israel!"

No wonder Ben-Gurion faced a storm in the State Council! But he too was adamant. "Rebel gangs can spell disaster for us. There is a truce, but no end to the war. We are fighting for our lives, I am no coward, but an armed group in our midst makes me afraid."

Bitterly he described a previous agreement that had been signed with the Irgun, and which Beigin had broken. He had to speak loudly to be heard against the murmurings and grumblings of his audience. Even in the State Council there were several who considered he had acted like a dictator.

Nevertheless, Ben-Gurion won the day. Much more, he showed Israel, and all the world, that he was a Prime Minister indeed. Unflinchingly he had faced a severe test of his authority. It strengthened his hand.

Ben-Gurion strode out of the council-chamber determined to drive the lesson home. Together with other members of his Government, he wrote out an oath of loyalty which he demanded that every man and woman in uniform swear. Haganah, descended from the old defence organisation of 1909 of which David Green, the young pioneer of Galilee, was one of the earliest members, now existed no more. It was abolished. So was the Palmach. Instead, every soldier became a member of the Defence Army of Israel, with proper Army ranks and absolute military discipline.

The oath said: "I swear on my honour to accept without question the discipline of the Defence Army, to obey all orders given by its Commanders, and to devote all my strength and, if need be, give my life in defence of my country and its freedom."

The Irgun soldiers jailed for their part in the *Altalena* affair were also given the chance to take the oath. Those who did so were released. The others were kept under lock and key.

The four weeks of truce, during which all these events happened, ended on July 9. The Arabs sprang to the offensive again, hoping this time to undo their mistakes and deliver a quick knock-out blow upon the Israeli forces.

How wrong they were! In a lightning, ten-day campaign, the Jews captured Lydda airport together with several neighbouring villages, entered Nazareth, bombed Cairo and Damascus, cut off the Egyptians from their bases and captured five thousand prisoners. They occupied a large part of the area supposed to form the new Arab state, and they pressed on to complete their victory by an assault on the Old City of Jerusalem.

This, however, was not to be. Count Bernadotte returned hurriedly from America, where he had been to report to the United Nations, and proclaimed another cease-fire. He refused to give this a time-limit. Then he sat down to plan a more lasting settlement between the opposing sides. There was a notion in his head that, if the Jews could be persuaded to give back some of their hard-won gains, the Middle East could carry on again as though nothing had happened. In particular, Bernadotte recommended to the United Nations that Israel should give up what it held of Jerusalem (that is, the New City) and the Negev.

Surrender our conquests now? thought the Jews. Never! After all, what had the United Nations done to safeguard the city which was not only holy to the great religions of the world, but also the home of a hundred thousand of their brothers? Nothing! How could Israel now abandon her people to the mercy of the Arab Legion after the United Nations had shown itself powerless?

When asked what he would do if he was told that Jerusalem could not remain within his state, Ben-Gurion replied: "The New City of Jerusalem is occupied territory. It stays with us until our enemies sit down and discuss peace."

So it has been ever since, for the Arabs refuse to sit down with the Jews. Jerusalem remains to this day a divided city. Sometimes, as the years went by, Ben-Gurion was urged by various foreign Governments to give up his section of it. But he has now decided that it will never happen. He has made it the capital of Israel, the seat of Government and the headquarters of the Zionist movement.

This was to come later. In those early months following what is termed the War of Independence, Jerusalem was kept somewhat apart, and as occupied territory it was ruled by a Military Governor. One day, in September, 1948, Count Bernadotte telephoned the Governor, saying he would like to come over for a discussion. The Swede then left his office to drive over to the Governor's house. Alas, he never reached his destination. An unknown assassin shot him down in the street.

Many Jews considered Bernadotte's views to be wrong, but they all agreed that he was a noble servant in the cause of peace. What a cruel and tragic end to a life spent on behalf of others! All Israel was ashamed.

Ben-Gurion was in Tel-Aviv when he heard the news. It saddened him to think that Jews could be guilty of such gangsterism, and he resolved to root out the 'disease' once and for all. The problem existed in Jerusalem rather than elsewhere, because it was not so easy to control the private armed organisations there, whose members had not sworn the oath of loyalty.

Menachem Beigin of the Irgun had nothing to do with the crime, but nevertheless Ben-Gurion sent him this angry message: "Disband your men, surrender your arms within twenty-four hours and submit to the laws of Israel, or the Army will act against you!"

Beigin obeyed. Then the Prime Minister ordered a hunt for all past and present members of the Stern Group and he put them behind bars. But to this day the police have not tracked down the killer of Bernadotte. He probably fled the country.

The war was all but over. The Egyptians, still rankling under the hammer-blows dealt them, took advantage of Ben-Gurion's worries about internal problems. They started to make a nuisance of themselves in the Negev despite the cease-fire, and interfered with convoys supplying the Jewish settlements there.

Once again, therefore, the Israelis were forced to

strike. First they captured Beersheba, then they pursued the enemy, now in headlong flight, across the border. There only remained now the Negev beachhead called Eilat on the Gulf of Akaba to complete the victory.

Ben-Gurion said to his chief of staff, General Yadin: "We must get to Eilat secretly, and occupy it before others step in."

"It will be quite a job, Mr. Ben-Gurion; there are no roads for us to use. But I have an idea."

"What is it?"

"Let's look at the Bible."

Closely they studied what the Bible said of journeys overland from the centre of Palestine to the Red Sea. General Yadin was an archaeologist, and could trace out the ancient routeways from the remains of past civilisations that had been dug out of the earth.

They found a track. It lay close to the Transjordan frontier. What many had done thousands of years before on foot or by camel they could do today in their jeeps. Yadin saluted his commander and departed. Two days later he sent a telegram to Ben-Gurion containing these three words—"Greetings from Eilat."

This rounded off a heroic chapter in Israel's story. Ben-Gurion's enemies had been brought to their knees. They gave up trying to destroy his state—for the time being, at any rate.

The Jew from Plonsk had proved to be a great war commander. But the plans he had for his country made the peace no less dramatic, as we shall see.

CHAPTER X

Building the State of Israel

WITHIN a very short time the Arabs had been soundly defeated and shamed before the entire world. Yet they still refused to face the fact that a state of Israel was now in being, and although they were forced to sign armistice agreements with it, they would not turn these into peace treaties. As a result, there was constant trouble on the borderlands. Sometimes this would take the form of an exchange of rifle-fire over the frontier, but there were times when the Arabs dared to go further, stealing across into Israel under cover of night to ambush people or steal cattle.

Naturally, the Jews were angered by this Arab attitude, particularly their Prime Minister, David Ben-Gurion. From time to time he issued stern warnings to his unfriendly neighbours, saying that Israel could not put up with this 'war of nerves', as it was called. When these warnings were of no avail, he ordered his troops to teach them a lesson. But the nuisance went on, and finally led to more serious trouble.

Having a 'war of nerves' on the border made the

task of building the country very difficult. For it meant keeping the Army in a constant state of readiness, and spending money on tanks and war-planes that might otherwise have been turned to a more useful purpose.

Nevertheless, the country's affairs were gradually put in order. Buses began to run regularly; schools were built; laws passed concerning taxes and health. There was so much to catch up on, for a war of life or death is not the best way to start a nation on its road to freedom.

In the meantime, the question arose as to who should be the first President of the state. In most people's minds there could be only one candidate for this high office: Dr. Chaim Weizmann.

The Zionist leader and world-famous scientist was seventy-four years old when Israel was created, and in failing health. Furthermore, age had brought the threat of blindness and he spent a great deal of time in America to consult his doctors. Yet he answered the call of his people, and was given a great welcome as he proceeded to his home in Rehovoth, close by the great scientific institute which bears his name.

Now all the trials and difficulties of past years were forgotten as Ben-Gurion embraced the man with whom he had worked side by side, in good times and bad, for so long. They had had their differences, these two, but in fact theirs had been a wonderful partnership, crowned with success.

One more name must be linked with these two in the triumph of Israel: Theodor Herzl. After Dr. Weizmann arrived to take up office as President, both he and Ben-Gurion decided that this was also the time to fulfil the dying wish of the man who will for ever be remembered as the father of the Jewish state. Herzl had asked that when the state became a reality, his remains should be taken to Israel for burial. Forty-five years later, in August, 1949, this was done. One of Ben-Gurion's closest colleagues in the Government, David Remez, travelled to Vienna with other Zionist leaders and high Army officers to bring the coffin to its resting-place. It was flown in an Israeli aircraft, and brought to Tel-Aviv, where it rested overnight. There, two hundred thousand people filed past to pay their respects. Then, wrapped in the flag of Israel, it was taken along the newly-built road which linked Tel-Aviv with Jerusalem. On the highest hill overlooking the city Ben-Gurion and his Cabinet Ministers were waiting. The coffin was lowered into the earth beside the graves of soldiers who had fallen in the War of Independence. Representatives from every town and village in Israel then came forward and placed hand-fuls of soil, tied in blue and white bags, in the grave. At the end of this moving ceremony the Prime Minister spoke.

"Throughout our long history," he said, "only two persons have had their remains brought by our own people, freed from bondage, into this land. Both were sons of Jacob: Joseph, whose bones were brought with the Israelite tribes freed from Egypt; and 3,300 years later, the son of Jacob Herzl is brought back, one year after the birth of the state."

And he added, as the great silent crowd gazed up at him standing on the crest of the hill: "We have witnessed not a funeral procession, but a victory parade."

Ben-Gurion loved to study the history of his people, so as to understand the present through knowing the past. Indeed, he never tired of talking history, especially to his closest admirers in the Government. There was nothing they could not learn from the Bible, he told them.

Who were those advisers? First there was the Foreign Minister, Moshe Shertok. He had been with Ben-Gurion in Turkey during the early days of Poale Zion, and now changed his name to the Hebrew one of Sharett. Eliezer Kaplan was appointed Minister of Finance, and David Remez Minister of Communications.

The most important of all Israel's problems was that of defending the country. For this reason the Prime Minister also took the office of Minister of Defence. He decided that every young citizen, man and woman, should serve in the armed forces. He developed the Navy and the Air Force. He put General Yadin in command of them.

"Yours is the most urgent task in all Israel," Ben-Gurion impressed upon the general. "By making these people good soldiers you will be turning them into good citizens also."

One of the first laws passed announced that every Jew had the right to come to Israel. What followed was one of the most inspiring happenings that any nation could boast. In the first year two hundred thousand came to the country. The European camps were emptied as young and old Jews made their way to the Holy Land. A welcome awaited them all. If they were strong and healthy, there was work in plenty to do. If they were sick or aged, they were received in hospitals or special homes.

They came from Poland, Rumania, Czechoslovakia, Bulgaria. Central Europe was almost emptied of its Jews, at least of those allowed to leave their own countries. But this was not all. There were Jews also in the Arab lands—devoted, pious people who had kept themselves apart through the centuries, almost unknown to the Jews of Europe.

Soon, down in the southernmost tip of Arabia, all along the North African coastline, in tiny villages of the Sahara desert, the word went round that a new King David had come to rule in Israel. Pious Oriental Jews felt they were living in the times of the Messiah. They came, sometimes in entire village groups, to take their place in the nation.

Thus it turned out just as Ben-Gurion had said. General Yadin enrolled them into the Army and had them educated in the Hebrew language. Some of them were unable to tie their bootlaces when they first arrived, for they were ignorant of footwear. Now, as they learnt their drill, the notion dawned upon them that they were the first generation of Israel's soldiers since the days of Bar-Cochba. What pride their uniforms gave them!

"The Holy Land is ancient, but we are living in the twentieth century," the Prime Minister reminded the nation. "This means that we must accomplish in a few years what others have spent decades in doing. We need industries, so we must train our people in new skills. We must export our goods in our own ships, and therefore we must become sailors. We must settle in the Negev, drain the marshlands, build roads and railways."

He called in scientific experts from abroad, and they took samples of Israel's soil to their laboratories to see what might be made to grow in it. Ben-Gurion had great faith in science. He especially believed that atomic energy could solve many of the country's problems; for it was a poor country, without the oil with which its neighbours were blessed, or other natural riches.

What science could not tell him, he found in his favourite book, the Bible. From it he learned that copper lay deep in the foothills of Timna, in the Negev. So he had his experts working down there, and they found copper. Just as the holy writings served him in war, they inspired him in peace. He knew that the Negev was once the scene of a great civilisation, but after many centuries of neglect it had become barren and empty. He had massive irrigation pipes constructed to lead water down from the north. He encouraged workers to settle in Beersheba and in Eilat.

"These are the finest pioneers of all," he once said after touring the kibbutzim and other villages in the wild south of Israel.

Ben-Gurion had other hopes for his country. One was the subject of constant discussion with his Foreign Minister, Moshe Sharett. It concerned Israel's place in the Asian continent. They both felt that the Jewish nation must hold out the hand of friendship even if it was spurned. As we have seen, the Arabs refused it. So their minds ranged farther afield, to the distant

E

nations of the East, such as India, China and Japan.

Being a scholar as well as a man of action, Ben-Gurion knew the writings of the ancient philosophers of those lands, just as he had taught himself all about the Greeks. They excited him, and he would often ask Sharett how he was getting on in forging close links with them.

"You must make Israel understood in the Far East," he would repeat. "Send some of our young men out there to explain what we're trying to do. We can become a bridge between East and West."

"I've already arranged for this," Sharett answered. "And as soon as I'm able, I shall travel those lands myself. They, too, are winning their freedom after centuries of foreign rule." Years later, after he had himself been Prime Minister, Sharett was able to keep his promise.

A man who carried a very heavy burden was Eliezer Kaplan, in charge of the Treasury. Now, as he observed Ben-Gurion at work on his ambitious plans, he grew anxious about their cost.

"We are plunging into bankruptcy," he reported. "Unless we move more slowly the money will dry up."

"I refuse to move slowly! We *must* bring our people in while there is time. Who knows if their Governments will allow them to leave next year, or the year after? They have waited two thousand years for this chance. And we *must* build up the Negev and settle our people there, or we may lose it."

"Then how do you propose to pay for it all?"

"The Jewish communities of the West will help us.

130

If they can't come here themselves, let them at least send us money."

"They already send us a great deal, Mr. Prime Minister."

Ben-Gurion observed the other in silence for a moment, and saw how Kaplan, a strong and burly man, looked tired and worn. Then he spoke. "My dear Eliezer, you and I have been through much together. We went through riots and bloodshed here. We fought for our rights at the Zionist Congress. Sometimes the struggle seemed hopeless. Yet we went on, building, building all the time. Did lack of money ever stop us?"

"True, it did not. But now we need more than ever before. We are forcing our people to shoulder heavy burdens. Taxes are high. Food is short. And it will take still more time before those who are now arriving are trained in useful work. Most of these immigrants are not used to hard manual labour on the land."

"Neither were we, when we first arrived. Remember those blisters on our palms, and the malaria? But our love for the country overcame every difficulty." Ben-Gurion began to grow impatient, as he always did when the subject of money was brought up. "We are not building Israel just for ourselves," he went on, his voice rising, "it is for all Jewry. If we are strong, the Jews in other countries will walk more proudly. That is why they must be ready to help."

"We require immense sums. Only the Jews of America are numerous and wealthy enough to raise so much."

"How much do you want from America?"

131

"At least five hundred million dollars during the next few years."

"Then why not float a loan? It will all be repaid when we are on our feet."

"It is possible, Mr. Prime Minister. But only you will be able to bring it off."

"I shall go."

Ben-Gurion went to America on this mission, in May, 1951. Together with his wife, he flew over in the first transatlantic flight of Israel's own airline. American Jewry gave him a hero's welcome such as has rarely been seen in that country.

As the man who had changed the course of Jewish history was driven along Broadway, the great thoroughfare in New York, nearly a million people crowded the pavements, waving flags and cheering. In Washington he was greeted by the President of the United States, Mr. Truman, who had always been a supporter of Zionism and was the first Head of State to accord the state of Israel official recognition. He spoke to a huge audience of twenty thousand at Madison Square Garden, and in his speech implored American Jews to help Israel to the utmost.

"Israel belongs to the Jews the world over," he said, his voice swelling as it reached through the microphone into every corner of that famous meeting-place. "Many hundreds of thousands look to us for hope. We do not want statehood for ourselves alone!"

He showed that more people had come into Israel during the first thirty months of freedom than in all the thirty years of British rule. The applause was terrific, especially when Ben-Gurion spoke of saving lives. Then thousands of people responded to the message by offering money so that the work might go on. And after New York, he visited the largest cities of the United States, achieving everywhere the same result.

Money was very necessary to help Israel along the road. But Ben-Gurion never regarded it as all-important. He wanted to see more Zionists come and settle in Israel, in addition to those who were persecuted in their old homes. Sometimes he became cross with his old comrades of the Zionist movement who, from afar, kept giving him advice on how to conduct the affairs of state.

"Of course we're making mistakes," he would tell them. "Ours is not an easy task. We're building a nation out of nothing, and we need all the help we can get. Come to Israel and join us!"

Only a few came. It was a cruel disappointment to Ben-Gurion, and indeed to all Israelis. This did not mean they did not welcome the Jews who made their homes in Israel because they had to flee from their misery in other lands. But they needed more doctors, engineers, teachers, particularly from the English-speaking world, to share their pioneering life.

Ben-Gurion hardly ever travelled abroad. His visit to America in 1951 was his only official visit to any foreign country. There was so much to occupy him at home. He spent a great deal of time encouraging the newcomers, because sometimes they were disheartened by their hardships, such as living in rough camp conditions until proper houses could be built. He also came very often to Parliament (its Hebrew name is Knesset), and when he did so, word soon got around and the members' benches and the visitors' gallery became crowded. Most of all, however, he loved to be with the Army, observing the soldiers in battle-training, or joining in their sing-songs at their barracks, or swapping stories with them about war-time experiences. Life was exciting in Israel and he made it seem more so, especially to the youth.

The country grew with a speed that dazzled the onlooker. Crops were sown in the Negev; Beersheba, a sleepy Turkish township when it was conquered by the Jews, became, in the space of a few years, a flourishing city. Great new factories for chemicals were built around Haifa Bay, new villages were dotted all around the borderlands.

How jealously the Arab rulers watched Israel's progress! They persuaded their people that they had plans to halt the work. "Soon we shall fight the second round," they claimed. "And when the time is ripe we shall throw out these intruders." They signed secret pledges to help each other to destroy Israel.

It was a dangerous state of affairs. Yet Ben-Gurion had plenty of other problems too. There was, for example, his old political enemy, Menachem Beigin. This man was now the leader of one of the Parliamentary groups, Herut (Freedom Party), and pretty powerful it was.

Beigin opposed Ben-Gurion tooth and nail. He blamed the country's money troubles on the fact that the Histadruth was now even stronger than it was before 1948. He preached to the new immigrants. He tried to form an alliance with other political parties.

He did not hide his opinion that Israel should take over the Old City of Jerusalem and that part of Palestine which lay beyond the Jordan.

On one occasion, early in 1952, Beigin whipped up so much feeling against the Prime Minister that there was a danger of the country being plunged into civil war. It occurred during a debate in the Knesset over whether Israel should accept payment from Germany to atone for the crimes committed against the Jews during Hitler's rule—the mass murders, the imprisonments, the seizure of property. The Government was in favour of doing so, but a bitter argument arose that divided the nation. People asked whether it was right to come to terms with a nation guilty of the greatest crimes in history.

A huge crowd assembled outside the Knesset as Ben-Gurion was speaking, and Beigin left his seat to go outside and stir it up. Police guarded the Parliament building as the crowd began to move up to its doors, as if to force an entrance. Tear gas was used by the police, and some of the demonstrators threw smoke bombs, so that the police had to use their batons to disperse the mob.

Smoke poured into the building, but Ben-Gurion sat through it all, even when Beigin himself returned to take part in the debate. There was an angry duel of words between the two, during which Ben-Gurion spoke with disgust of "those hooligans in the streets".

"You are the hooligan!" Beigin called back. The Speaker ordered Beigin out for insulting a fellow-member of Parliament. As he left, the Herut leader shouted: "We are ready to die rather than deal with the Germans. We shall fight at the barricades!"

Nevertheless the Government won the day, and all was quiet again in the streets. But the Prime Minister would not forgive Beigin for his rebellious behaviour. In the course of a broadcast to the nation he warned Beigin that Israel would not put up with such methods, or bow to threats.

"I know that it is not so difficult to carry out acts of murder against members of the Government," he said. "I know I am the chief target of Beigin's plans. It is my duty to tell the nation: do not panic and do not be afraid. The army, the police and the people will see that this insane plot will not succeed. I shall not tolerate threats against the freedom of the state."

These were strong words, but everyone knew that the man who sank the *Altalena* meant what he said. Evidently Beigin thought the better of it, too, for the German agreement was signed and there was no revolt.

Yes, Ben-Gurion's was no easy job. He was now sixty-six, yet despite his snowy hair he was robust in body and mind. He and his wife Paula lived simply in their official home in Jerusalem. They did not even have servants. They behaved, in fact, like ordinary citizens.

Every man hugs a special dream to himself, and now Ben-Gurion had one. It was to retire from public life, to give him more time with his books, and the peace and quiet to think about the great problems of the state. He discussed this idea with his wife.

"I must take a rest from politics," he told Paula.

"Perhaps if I went away the differences between the parties in the Knesset would heal."

"Yes, David. You've been in the thick of things for too long. It will do Israel good to get along without you for a while."

But when he discussed the subject with his closest advisers, such as the wise Rabbi Maimon or his military assistant, Colonel Argov, they were taken aback.

"You can't retire yet," they said. "Israel is too young a child to be without its father. Who is there to take your place?"

"I *will* give up my office soon," Ben-Gurion replied with determination. "It isn't good for a country to rely on one man. In the old days, at the Jewish Agency, there was Weizmann to share our problems with me. But now he's too ill to bear these burdens."

This was true. Although it seemed impossible to think of the Jewish world without him, the President was now nearing the end of his life. A report of his health was telephoned to the Prime Minister's office every day. Joseph Sprinzak, the Speaker of the Knesset, acted as his deputy at every important event. With heaviness in its heart, the nation awaited the worst. Weizmann's name carried with it the same magic as Herzl's half a century before. He was above politics. Even the Herut party accepted him as President while they rebelled against Ben-Gurion as Prime Minister.

On December 9, 1952, Dr. Weizmann died. As the Speaker announced the news to the members of the Knesset, there were tears in his eyes. At the funeral

Ben-Gurion described Weizmann as the greatest Jew of their time.

Nevertheless, nations have to carry on. A new President had to be found. And because this man had to be elected by the Knesset, everybody knew that Mapai, the leading party in the state, would make the decision. And this meant it would be Ben-Gurion's decision, for the party would not act in any matter of importance against his advice.

Several names were discussed. The man who seemed the most obvious choice was Sprinzak. But Ben-Gurion had other ideas. He considered the Speaker to be too closely bound up with politics to be the most suitable Presidential candidate. He wanted this highest of all offices to be free of politics.

Ben-Gurion's mind went back to the year before, when he was in America. There he had had a long meeting with Albert Einstein, the great mathematician and physicist. The Israeli Prime Minister felt a great admiration for Einstein, who was a Jew and had been driven out of Germany by Hitler. Why not Einstein as successor to Weizmann?

Ben-Gurion sent him a letter offering him the office. "No Jew could have a greater honour than to be President of Israel," he wrote. "You are the most illustrious of all living Jews."

Einstein refused. He excused himself on the grounds that he was unsuitable. Ben-Gurion was bitterly disappointed, for he thought there was more than just this in the refusal. It told him that the Jews of the world simply did not understand, or did not wish to understand, the great historic importance to them of the rebirth of Israel, as well as to the Jews residing in the country.

But wait! Surely there lived here, in Jerusalem, a modest scholar, a faithful warrior in the Zionist struggle, a man who had never asked for anything for himself, but was as worthy of honour as any? Yes, the tall youth David Green had met in Jaffa in 1907, who had been his comrade in the days of *Hashomer*, his fellow-editor of the workers' newspaper and fellow-prisoner under the Turks, and then his fellow-exile.

Ben-Gurion strode quickly over to the wooden house, just a few minutes' walking-distance from his own, where Isaac Ben-Zvi lived.

"You have served the Jewish people well," said the Prime Minister, "and I know you now wish to rest. But there is one more task that you can perform better than any of us, and I implore you to accept it."

Ben-Zvi now spent his time in study and writing books. Standing beside him as his visitor talked was his wife, once known as Rachel Yanait. After a minute's pause he replied: "If you wish me to be the new President I will agree."

Of course, Ben-Zvi was elected, to become even more loved by all his people, as one devoted to their well-being.

Ben-Gurion was happy now to revive the partnership that had achieved so much in earlier years. Once again it proved fruitful. The state grew swiftly. Many foreigners came to review its progress; famous authors from abroad came to write about it; films describing how much a free Jewish nation could accomplish were shown in many countries.

Then, once again, Ben-Gurion felt the old times tug at his memory. He recalled the pioneering days in Petach Tikva, and in Kfar Saba, and in Galilee. Israel needed that pioneering spirit still—perhaps more so, now. The rugged Negev awaited a peaceful conquest by the sweat of manual labour, by hands that would work with love for the soil and make it blossom as the rose.

Now he made up his mind, despite all efforts to dissuade him, to go down to the Negev himself. He would hand over the reins of his heavy office to another faithful comrade, Moshe Sharett, and join the brave young pioneers there.

Of course, the Government and many other leading citizens begged him to remain. But he was adamant. "My spirit is weary," he informed them. "I shall go to Sde Boker, one of our remotest settlements. This is the Zionism of today—the practical work of up-building, not the conflicts of politicians."

So Paula and David Ben-Gurion travelled to that tiny village in the wilderness, forty miles south-west of Beersheba. He gave up his powerful position as Prime Minister to make the entire world gasp in wonder, and the ageing statesman of nearly seventy settled down once again to the simple life of the shepherd.

CHAPTER ELEVEN

Man of Peace, Man of Action

THE little settlement had been founded only a year and a half before David and Paula Ben-Gurion came to join it. A group of young men and women, comrades in the firing-line during the War of Independence, were its pioneers. They had banded together and decided to exchange city-life for the Negev. Packing a few belongings, they first made for Beersheba. Then they had followed an old camel-path until they came to what appeared to be a suitable place to rear sheep.

It had no name. No one had lived there since the Romans had left in the seventh century. But they knew that the Bedouin sometimes grazed their flocks near by. So they determined to make this their home.

"We'll call this place Sde Boker, 'the Field of the Herdsman,'" they decided, and proceeded to pitch their tents.

Within the first few weeks, two of their number— a youth and a girl—fell victim to a sniper's bullet. But they stayed on, working quietly away, bringing water, building huts, sowing their crops.

141

No special fuss was made of the Ben-Gurions when they arrived, except that they were granted the privilege of a three-roomed hut for themselves. One of the rooms housed the former Prime Minister's library. The other two were bedrooms; Paula's was converted into a sitting-room every day. They took their meals with the others, in the communal dining-hall.

Ben-Gurion knew the life was going to be hard. He had once said in a speech: "It is difficult to be a worker. It is a hundred times more difficult to be a Jewish worker. It is a thousand times more difficult to be a Jewish worker in the land of Israel."

Now, at sixty-eight years of age, and after a lifetime of toiling to give his people the chance to become workers in their own land, he would remind his people that these were not mere empty phrases. He would be a Jewish worker in the toughest part of this country, a part which must be conquered and brought under the plough just as Galilee was conquered thirty years before.

Every morning he worked for four hours, wheeling barrows of fodder, cleaning the cattle-stalls, tending the sheep. Paula did her turn of duty in the dining-hall, then helped in the sick-room, for she was a trained nurse.

In the afternoons and evenings Ben-Gurion was to be found among his books, reading, writing or studying his favourite subject—ancient philosophy. He wrote all his letters by hand. His other writings were sent to Tel-Aviv to be typed. Then they were posted to newspapers all over the world, to be translated into several languages.

Sde Boker, from being an almost unknown pioneering outpost, became world-famous. Films were made of life in the village. Important visitors drove down by jeep to meet the Prime Minister who was now a shepherd.

Freed from office, he had time now to think out the great problems of the day: world politics, science and religion, the future of the Zionist movement. He was very outspoken about all these, sometimes to the annoyance of people in high places.

For example, a few weeks after he had settled down in his desert home he received an invitation to address an important Zionist meeting in Jerusalem. Leaders from many countries had come together to discuss their work, and they wanted to have the former Prime Minister's views.

He refused the invitation, and in a curt letter made no secret of his opinion that such discussions were largely a waste of time. Why did they need to discuss the meaning of Zionism? In his mind a Zionist was a Jew who came to live in Israel, otherwise he was no different from other Jews who helped Israel. No, it was more useful to labour at Sde Boker than to address a Zionist meeting in Jerusalem.

This was a rebuff indeed, and it echoed throughout the Jewish world. But Ben-Gurion did not spare those living in Israel either. If they slackened, he told them so. "A homeland cannot be bought with money or conquered by the sword," he scolded. "It has to be created with toil and sweat, and if necessary defended with one's life!"

He was worried because his people seemed to carry

their political differences to extremes of bitterness, and therefore spared no thought for the toil and sweat. Not enough young people were coming to the Negev. It was there that true Zionism could be lived.

One day Ben-Gurion received a telephone call. The Minister of Education was on the line from Jerusalem. "Your views must be heard by our children," said the Minister. "They are the leaders of the future. Next month the children from every top class of every high school will be coming to a great rally, and I should be honoured if you will come and address them."

Ben-Gurion loved children. They often seemed to him wiser than their parents. "Where is the meeting?" he asked.

"At Sheikh Munis, just north of Tel-Aviv. There'll be nearly ten thousand youngsters, seated in a great circle in the open air."

"I'll come."

Despite the fact that it meant leaving a hospital bed, because of an attack of lumbago, Ben-Gurion would not break this appointment. A deafening cheer greeted his arrival as, simply dressed in khaki shirt and trousers, he hobbled on to the platform with the aid of a stick. Then there was absolute silence as thousands of pairs of eyes feasted themselves on the man who was already a legend.

Once he began to speak, Ben-Gurion forgot his aches and pains. The children were enthralled as he thundered against soft living at a time of great difficulties for the state. His theme was unity—unity between the old settlers and the newcomers, unity between all workers, unity for defence.

"Our War of Independence was the first time in our history that Jewish blood was not spilt in vain. But we must realise that our victory wasn't final. The struggle against our enemies is not yet over. Furthermore," he told the vast audience, "not enough people understand how bad it is for the country that many thousands of newcomers are not yet fixed up with proper homes, but have to live in makeshift shelters. Also, the borderlands cannot be properly guarded against a possible invader if our youth does not go and settle in the new villages on the frontier."

Ben-Gurion repeated these words to other meetings of young people up and down the country. Many of his hearers disagreed with him, or thought he was asking too much of the nation. But all regarded him with admiration and love. For Ben-Gurion became the 'conscience' of Israel, and young and old looked to him for guidance just as an individual might look into his own conscience.

The year 1954 was a grim one for Israel. Border violence was taking its cruel toll of young pioneers; relations with the Arab Powers grew steadily worse; an Israeli ship was seized while trying to pass through the Suez Canal; and, to cap it all, there was a change of Government in Egypt, and soon a new dictator, Nasser, was on the scene, anxious to prove himself as the champion of the Arabs.

Matters were not helped when this man received large supplies of military equipment from abroad, sent to him by Western statesmen who were worried lest Egypt might turn away from them and towards Communism. For the stronger Egypt and the other

Arab countries became, the more difficult was it for Israel to keep abreast. Money she could ill afford had to be spent on planes and guns wherever she could get them, and at whatever the price.

Little wonder, then, that Prime Minister Moshe Sharett sent an urgent message to his old chief in Sde Boker.

"The country needs you and wants you back," he wrote. "Will you join my Government as Minister of Defence? You are the one who created our army. I should be grateful if you would take charge of it again, for we may have to use it suddenly."

It was an offer Ben-Gurion could not resist. Although a man of peace, he was deeply proud of the Jewish soldiers who had so gallantly defended the state in its first days.

"Accepted! I'll leave for Jerusalem at once."

In February, 1955, Ben-Gurion was back in the Government, after one year and two months at Sde Boker. But he would not give up his desert home completely. He returned to the 'Field of the Herdsman' again and again, to show he belonged there as much as anywhere in Israel.

The old warrior's come-back was a worry to the country's enemies. It was known that he never shirked a duty; and the need of the hour was to make the Army ready for any test.

From the moment he got back into harness there was a new spirit of defiance in the nation. As Minister of Defence, Ben-Gurion made it his duty to warn his neighbours that Israel would not put up with the constant raids across her borders. But the new master of Egypt, Nasser, grew more boastful every day.

"There will be a second round against Israel," he promised the jostling Cairo crowds. "When we are ready we shall crush the Zionists." And, to show that he meant these words, he visited other Arab capitals to sign a pact of war against Israel.

Ben-Gurion's answer to these moves was: "I am ready to meet Nasser anywhere, any time, to improve relations between us. We can be friends. But if we are attacked, let the world know that we shall destroy the Egyptians."

No one in Israel, nor outside for that matter, took these to be empty phrases. There was no reason why Israel should welcome a war, every reason why she should have peace. But as time wore on, the Israelis were convinced that the "second round" would surely come.

"Arab loathing of the Jews is so great that any talk of peace is foolish," exclaimed Nasser. He recruited specially trained men to steal across the frontier into Israel, spread terror by acts of murder, and then escape back to their bases. These bands were known as 'Fedayeen', and were made up of fanatical haters of the Jews. Sometimes they were daring enough to penetrate deep into Israel territory, disguising themselves as Bedouin so as to reach safety over the Jordan frontier on the other side of the country. Many of them were captured. These prisoners confessed that their plan was to create confusion and fear in Israel by every possible means.

It happened in the Negev. It happened in Jerusalem.

The whole nation had the feeling of being in the front line.

Because of these dangers, people looked to Ben-Gurion rather than to the Prime Minister, Moshe Sharett, as their leader. Although Sharett was admired greatly for his skill and wisdom as a statesman who brought great credit to Israel, he was not the man to lead it in this time of danger. Sharett realised this, too. He did not think that he and Ben-Gurion made a good team.

There was a General Election in Israel in July, 1955, and Sharett decided that if Ben-Gurion would take his place, this was a suitable moment for him to give up his post as Prime Minister. As was his duty, he went to see the President.

"My advice to you is to ask Mr. Ben-Gurion to form a new Government," he said.

Ben-Zvi summoned Ben-Gurion in August, 1955. "I entrust you with the task of forming a Government," he said. "In the face of our growing difficulties, this must be completed without delay."

Of course, there was no doubt that Ben-Gurion, refreshed after his retirement, welcomed the chance to be fully in charge of his country's destiny once again. He kept his old post of Minister of Defence also, while Sharett went back to *his* old post—Foreign Minister.

Just a few weeks later, the people of Israel received a new shock when they looked at their morning newspapers. The headlines told them that Egypt, dissatisfied with the flow of armaments that was coming to her from Western countries, had signed a new arms agreement with Czechoslovakia. This gave her every kind of modern weapon required for the waging of full-scale war.

An extremely serious situation thus arose, for Czechoslovakia was, of course, closely allied with Russia. She was, in fact, a kind of springboard from which Russia leapt right into Middle East affairs, with the chief purpose of opposing the influence of America and Britain there.

Stunned by the news, Israel waited to see what its Prime Minister would do about it. Ben-Gurion thought it wisest to tell his worst fears. "Unless we receive arms in sufficient quantities for our defence," he warned his countrymen, "it is almost certain that the Egyptian dictator will attack us in the next few months."

But where to get those arms? Ben-Gurion appealed to all the leading countries of the West for help. The Powers were completely taken by surprise by Russia's move into what they always considered their own 'sphere of influence', and had no policy to confront it. So they replied with promises, not with weapons—at least not with sufficient weapons to oppose the up-to-date jet planes, submarines and tanks that Egypt now had. The position grew blacker still.

Then one country, secretly at first, but later openly, answered the call for help. This was France. She had her own troubles with the Arabs of her North African empire, and had as much cause to distrust Nasser as Israel had. France had an Arab revolt on her hands in Algeria, and she saw in Israel a useful new ally on the Mediterranean seashore.

From this moment an arms race was on in all its fury. Some Russian officers arrived in the Nile Valley to train the Egyptian Army. Others were posted to the headquarters of Egypt's close ally, Syria. Israel's generals flew over to Paris for talks at the War Ministry and to tour the aircraft factories.

The French had an extremely efficient fighter plane, called the Mystère. Several squadrons were ordered for Israel, to be held in reserve should the Egyptians decide to use their new, high-flying Russian bombers against Tel-Aviv and other cities, which were just a few minutes by jet-plane from the Egyptian bases.

Ben-Gurion did not deceive himself about Israel's chances. He knew that his forces were not equal in fire-power to the Egyptians, but he was convinced that his soldiers could make up in quality and devotion what they lacked in quantity. The Arabs had nothing to defend but their masters; the Israelis had at heart the cause of safeguarding their precious, newly-won homeland.

In any case, as he kept telling his people, should the test come there was no way of retreat. Israel was but ten miles across at its narrowest, while Nasser brought his forces far east of the Nile, building great bases in the Sinai Peninsula and the strip of Palestine that he controlled around Gaza.

In July, 1956, Nasser felt strong enough to seize the Suez Canal Company, until then in the hands of the British and French Governments. This particularly angered the British Prime Minister, Sir Anthony Eden. He suddenly realised what Guy Mollet, the French Prime Minister, had been saying a long time: that

Nasser aimed to clear the Middle East of all Western influence.

What about the oil? worried Sir Anthony, in a panic. What about the freedom of shipping in the Suez Canal, a vital route for European trade to India and Australia? As a warning to Nasser, he moved British troops and ships of the Royal Navy as near to Suez as he could get them—Cyprus and Malta.

Ben-Gurion felt they were all approaching zero hour. He called his Chief of Staff, who was now the one-eyed general Moshe Dayan, to secret discussions at which he would permit no other person to be present, not even members of his Government. A special messenger hastened to Guy Mollet, the French Prime Minister. From these discussions emerged a plan, a desperate plan, to save Israel. This was to destroy the Egyptian threat by sending every possible man and gun into an attack upon Gaza and Sinai, before the ambitious Nasser struck first.

Late in October, 1956, General Dayan, speaking from his secret headquarters in the field, telephoned the Prime Minister, who was in Tel-Aviv. But he could not get through. The Prime Minister's military secretary answered the telephone instead. "*Hazaken* [i.e. the "old man", the expression by which his closest friends described Ben-Gurion] is sick. He has a high temperature and is not allowed to leave his bed."

"Tell him our mobilisation is complete. I am awaiting orders."

The next morning his temperature had fallen slightly, but Ben-Gurion still could not leave his bed. However, he had a constant stream of callers, bringing urgent State papers. One of these was from London—a message from Sir Anthony Eden.

This said that news of the Israeli mobilisation had reached the British Government. Such a step, the message went on, could only mean one thing—an attack upon an ally of Britain's, Jordan. Sir Anthony sternly announced that, should Israel use her troops against Jordan, Britain would fight on the Arab side.

The message made no reference to Egypt. This was not so strange, because Sir Anthony had plans of his own in that direction.

October 29 was a Monday. Doctors were still hovering around Ben-Gurion's bedside. They dosed him with medicines, but he proved a bad patient. For his mind was not on his sickness. In his hand was a map of the great expanse of desert known as Sinai that separated his country from Egypt proper. As the day wore on he grew restless, and at last, with an impatient wave of the hand, he dismissed the doctors.

The sick-room became a G.H.Q. In the early evening a signal was received stating that Israel's parachutists were dropping from the skies in Sinai and taking up positions within twenty miles of the Suez Canal. The wedge of desert reaching into the Red Sea was split in two. It was war.

General Dayan sent an Order of the Day to his troops. "Today our forces will break the suffocating ring of the Egyptian enemy," it ran. "Today our southern forces will tear to pieces the enemy's strongholds and bases which threaten Israel's border and her population. They will fight across the border and enclose the Egyptians in their own country."

And so it was. During the succeeding four days one hammer-blow followed another and brought havoc to Nasser's army. After the paratroops came the land forces. In a broad armoured column they shot across the desert from the Negev, capturing whole depots of equipment and taking thousands of prisoners.

The entire world watched fascinated as another crack force swung into El Arish from the rear, and sealed off the coast road from the fleeing enemy. The spearhead of this force then turned northwards, and by keeping to the coast occupied Rafa and Gaza, receiving the surrender of a general and reducing the Egyptian headquarters to a crumbling ruin.

Tanks were captured in their dozens; those that could not be brought back to the Israeli lines were destroyed. Dog-fights in the air brought the famous planes of Russian manufacture crashing to the ground.

Such was the situation on land and in the air. What was happening at sea? There, Nasser was having even worse luck. He sent a destroyer to shell Haifa harbour on the Wednesday, third day of the campaign. As the first shells began to drop uselessly into the bay, Naval and Air Force units went into action. The fight was over in half an hour. The battered and leaking ship limped into harbour, flying the white flag of surrender. The crew of 250 depressed Egyptians were marched to the nearest prison-cage.

General Dayan had one more job to do before he could claim possession of all Sinai. He had based a large detachment of troops at Eilat. Their brigade commander now received the signal he had been hourly expecting. It was to capture the southernmost tip of the peninsula and occupy the tiny islands that controlled the Red Sea traffic. This operation involved units on land, at sea and in the air. Yet it went like clockwork.

The Sinai campaign was over. That wilderness, known to all mankind because of the exodus of the Israelites four thousand years before, and where the Law had been entrusted to their keeping, was now the conquered territory of the wanderers' descendants.

Some twenty million pounds' worth of booty found its way back to Israel: a hundred tanks, a thousand trucks and military vehicles and two hundred guns. About three thousand Egyptians were killed and seven thousand taken prisoner. The Israelis lost 150 killed.

Meanwhile, what was Britain's attitude to this remarkable exploit of war, which in the space of little more than a hundred hours had resulted in the conquest of an area three times the size of Israel itself?

While the Israeli forces pressed forward, with the prospect, it seemed, of having all Egypt within their grasp, Sir Anthony sent an ultimatum to both sides. Speaking on behalf of France as well as his own country, he demanded that each withdraw to a line ten miles distant from either side of the Suez Canal. He stated also that British and French units would occupy the three main Canal towns of Port Said, Ismailia and Suez, by force if necessary.

Israel agreed, Egypt refused. Then the bombers of those two great European Powers took off from Cyprus and went into massive attack. They destroyed almost the whole of Nasser's air force. They sent in their troops just as Dayan's men were mopping up behind the ultimatum line.

Then the United Nations stepped in to prevent Sir Anthony from achieving all that he had hoped. There was a cease-fire, but in the eyes of many people the British Prime Minister had put himself in the wrong. Both America and Russia, for example, warned him that he was risking a world war, not so much to stop bloodshed between Egypt and Israel, but to get back his lost position in the Middle East.

The British and French soldiers soon withdrew to their bases in Cyprus. But what of the Israelis? Ben-Gurion had been prevented by his illness from being with his army in the field. But immediately afterwards he went, in spite of the displeasure of his doctors, to the Knesset. Paula Ben-Gurion waited anxiously as, brushing aside the offer of a chair, he stood for forty-five minutes to make one of the most important speeches of his career.

The Parliamentary building had not a seat to spare as he surveyed the results of the Sinai campaign. He showed that Israel had fought for reasons that were quite different from those of Britain and France.

"This has been the biggest and most glorious military campaign in the history of our people," he declared, "and one of the most wonderful military operations in world history. Our forces did not advance upon the territory of Egypt, and did not attempt to do so—just the Sinai peninsula."

With those opening words he gave the world a clue to his intentions. For he went on to say that the armistice agreement signed with Egypt at the end of

the War of Independence was dead and buried—
destroyed by Nasser's obstinate refusal to honour it.
He also said that Israel would not allow a foreign
force to occupy the territory she had conquered.
Israel would stay in Gaza and Sinai until Nasser
signed peace with her, a proper peace that allowed
Israel to carry on her work unhindered.

The Knesset members cheered. The people in the
streets cheered. All were confident in the justice of
their cause. They were glad that their leader intended
to stand firm.

But by the following day Ben-Gurion, from a happy
man, had become a sorrowing one. He had received
urgent letters from President Eisenhower of the U.S.A.
and Prime Minister Bulganin of Russia which, though
polite, were in fact blunt warnings. Israel must give
up her conquests. Or else . . .

The whole of the day Ben-Gurion spent debating
with himself. Should he bow to these warnings? What
would his people, who had suffered murder and pil-
lage all these years, think of him? And if he resisted,
what then? The Russians were trying desperately to
save Nasser. They might well take drastic action
against Israel—perhaps use their bombers on her
cities. What could he say to his gallant soldiers if he
had to undo their well-deserved victories?

These were the conflicting ideas in his mind. At
last he made his decision. But it was such a painful
one that he took the rare step of informing his people,
over the radio, of how he had come to it.

At nine o'clock on Thursday evening, November 8,
little more than a week after the first paratroops had

landed in Sinai, the Israeli radio programme was interrupted. It was announced that the Prime Minister would speak to the nation at midnight. All Israel waited for his speech.

When midnight came, the announcer said there would be a short delay, as the Prime Minister was not quite ready. Half an hour later, David Ben-Gurion, his voice sounding weary, came on the air. He told the whole story of the visits he had had from foreign Ambassadors, the letters received, the pressing messages from the United Nations. Yes, he had decided that, to safeguard the peace of the world and to uphold the rule of the United Nations, he must withdraw his troops.

Heavy of heart, the nation of Israel went to sleep that night, the soldiers in their camps, the pioneers in the kibbutzim, the new immigrants, the old settlers. They were not angry with their leader. They were with him, for his speech was the act of a courageous man. Only one who was really unafraid could have gone back on his word at such a time, and to a people in such a mood. As Ben-Gurion himself put it, how much Israel had won, and how much lost, only the future could tell.

As we near the end of this story of a great Jewish leader and a remarkable world statesman, let us think of him as he would wish, a man of peace. He hates bloodshed and he hates oppression, though he has lived in a land on the brink of war since the day it became a state; and in the midst of an Arab world where the poor are oppressed because of the self-pride and rivalry of their masters.

"What are your hopes for Israel in the next ten years?" a foreign correspondent asked him just before the tenth anniversary of the founding of the state.

"I see Israel growing by a million more people," Ben-Gurion replied. "They will come to us from all corners of the earth, to join in the wonderful adventure of our rebirth."

"What are your plans for these people? How will they live, in this tiny country?"

"We shall build new ports to export our goods to the world. One will be on the Mediterranean coast, the other at Eilat on the Red Sea. We shall serve as a link between the ancient world and the modern. The waters of the River Jordan will be brought south to make the deserts of the Negev fruitful. Here, many of our people will transform the Negev into a place of cities, factories and farms."

The questioner persisted: "What else do you expect of your people?"

The Prime Minister gazed through the window of his Tel-Aviv home, at the hurrying crowds that once were Poles, Persians, South Africans, Yemenites, Hungarians, but now were one nation, speaking one language. "I see this country and this people setting an example to the world, showing how men and women can learn to work together for the good of all."

The journalist put away his notebook, and rose to leave. "Come and see us again," Ben-Gurion said, as they parted with a friendly handshake. "You will be welcome."

Within a few weeks Israel was 'invaded' by hundreds of such journalists. For the young state was on the point of celebrating a very important occasion: its first decade of freedom. Every town and village was bedecked with flags, and excitement mounted as April 24, 1958, the actual anniversary according to the Roman calendar, drew near.

Ben-Gurion issued a special anniversary message to the Jews of the world. "Israel was established not only by the Jews who live within the state," it said, "and not for them alone; but by the Jewish nation of all generations, and for the Jewish people in all countries."

And as if to prove the truth of those words, many thousands of Jews came to Israel to share the happy holiday feeling of the celebrations. Hotels were packed. Students came and were billeted in camps and hostels. The kibbutzim opened their hospitable gates to accommodate the visitors. Private families took them into their homes.

The theme of the celebration was "Peace"—for Israel, for Jewry and for all mankind. But peace, Israel knew to her sorrow, was not yet come. While working for friendship and harmony with her neighbours, she had to be prepared for war. This was why vast masses of people, many of them tourists, crowded into Jerusalem to be in time to see the great military parade that was the centre of the pageantry of independence.

What a spectacle this proved to be! Giant tanks rumbled at the head, to be followed by naval contingents, paratroopers, women soldiers, frontier guardsmen. Proudly they marched past the platform and obeyed the command "Eyes Right!" where those two old comrades-in-arms and fellow-labourers in peace,

Isaac Ben-Zvi and David Ben-Gurion, took the salute.

During the day crowds flocked to the synagogues, and there was dancing all night long in the streets. Congratulations were sent by Sir Winston Churchill and President Eisenhower, as well as by many other famous statesmen. And the President and Mrs. Ben-Zvi gave a tea party to the 112 children who had been born on the same day as the state and were also ten years old.

The joy echoed round the world. In almost every city where Jews lived, and were free to rejoice, there were celebrations. In London, at the Royal Albert Hall; in New York, at the great Polo Grounds; in Paris and in Amsterdam and in Johannesburg—millions of Jews gave thanks for the safe arrival of the state of Israel among the nations.

And in all their hearts, there was a thought that day for the weather-beaten pilot who stood at the helm in Jerusalem, a modern prophet of Israel, a builder and a thinker.

Their greetings went out to David Ben-Gurion, the lad from the Polish ghetto who became the first Prime Minister of the first Jewish state for two thousand years; to the man who had dared all and raised the banner of Jewish freedom because of the faith he drew from the Bible and the courage it gave him to clasp the sword.